Foundations
for Adult Reading

Lifelong Learning Books
Scott, Foresman and Company
Glenview, Illinois   London

Special thanks to William C. Schick

Text Acknowledgments

15 "Because" from *Cotton Candy on a Rainy Day* by Nikki Giovanni. Copyright © 1978 by Nikki Giovanni. Reprinted by permission of William Morrow and Company, Inc. **22** Adapted, excerpted, and reprinted by permission of Joan Daves. Copyright © 1963 by Martin Luther King, Jr. **27** From *No Way of Knowing: Dallas Poems* by Myra Cohn Livingston. Copyright © 1980 by Myra Cohn Livingston. All Rights Reserved. Reprinted by permission of Marian Reiner for the author. **27** Copyright 1932 by Alfred A. Knopf, Inc. and renewed 1960 by Langston Hughes. Reprinted from *The Dream Keeper and Other Poems* by Langston Hughes, by permission of Alfred A. Knopf, Inc. **31–32** Zibby Oneal, *Grandma Moses: Painter of Rural America.* New York: Viking Penguin Inc., 1986. **48** Copyright 1926 by Alfred A. Knopf, Inc. and renewed 1954 by Langston Hughes. Reprinted from *Selected Poems of Langston Hughes* by permission of Alfred A. Knopf, Inc. **51–52** Adapted by permission of Random House, Inc. from *The American Medical Association Family Medical Guide.* Copyright © 1982 by The American Medical Association. **59–60** Adapted by permission of Random House, Inc. from *Wonder Women of Sports* by Betty Millsaps Jones. Copyright © 1981 by Random House, Inc. **67** Copyright 1923 by Holt, Rinehart and Winston and renewed 1951 by Robert Frost. Reprinted from *The Poetry of Robert Frost* edited by Edward Connery Lathem, by permission of Henry Holt and Company, Inc. **77** From *My Song Is a Piece of Jade* by Toni de Gerez. Copyright © 1981 and English translation © 1984 by Organizacion Editorial Novaro, SA. By permission of Little, Brown and Company. **81–82, 85, 88** Adapted from "Sons and gangs" by Lynn Emmerman from the *Chicago Tribune* (Jan. 22, 1989). Copyright © 1989 by Lynn Emmerman. Reprinted by permission of Lynn Emmerman. **93** "The Surrender Speech of Chief Joseph," 1877. **103–104** "Rice and Rose Bowl Blues" by Diane Mei Lin Mark from *Breaking Silence: Anthology of Contemporary Asian American Poets.* Copyright © 1983 by The Greenfield Review Press. Reprinted by permission of Diane Mei Lin Mark. **111–112** Adapted from "New Branches . . . Distant Roots" by Elzbieta Gozdziak from "Aging" (No. 359, 1989). Reprinted by permission of Elzbieta Gozdziak. **115–116, 120–121, 124–125** From *The New Americans* by Al Santoli. Copyright © Al Santoli, 1988. All rights reserved. Reprinted by permission of Viking Penguin, a division of Penguin Books USA Inc.

Authors

Sharon Fear

Mary K. Hawley

Luz Nuncio Schick

Consulting Editor

John Strucker
Adult Basic Education Teacher
Community Learning Center
Cambridge, Massachusetts

Foundations Consultants

Don Brunn
Instructor
Downtown Community College Center
San Francisco, California

Geneva Burden
Executive Director
Georgia Literacy Coalition, Inc.
Atlanta, Georgia

Charmaine M. Carney
Instructor/Coordinator
Independent Learning Center
Hawkeye Institute of Technology
Waterloo, Iowa

Mary S. Charuhas
Associate Dean of Adult Continuing Education
and Extension Services
College of Lake County
Grayslake, Illinois

Kathy Cooper
Training Coordinator
Washington Literacy
Seattle, Washington

Betty Gottfried
Teacher/Teacher Trainer
Adult Basic Education Agency Services
New York, New York

Leann Howard
Adult Basic Education/English as a Second
Language Resource Instructor
San Diego Community Colleges
Continuing Education Centers
San Diego, California

Shirley Huey
Program Director
Literacy Volunteers of Orange County Schools/
Literacy Volunteers of America in Central
Florida
Orlando, Florida

Valerie Meyer, Ph.D.
Associate Professor
Department of Curriculum and Instruction
Southern Illinois University at Edwardsville
Edwardsville, Illinois

Jill Plaza
Director
Reading and Educational Consultants
Palatine, Illinois

John H. Redd, Ed.D.
Retired Director of Adult Basic Education
Dallas Independent School District
Dallas, Texas

Gail Rice
Adult Basic Education Teacher
Palos Heights, Illinois

Kathy Roskos
Assistant Professor
Department of Education
John Carroll University
University Heights, Ohio

Contents

How to Use This Book

Foundations for Adult Reading 2 is a book to help you read and enjoy reading. It tells what to *do* as you read. You will learn to use what you already know as you read. You will learn to look ahead. You will learn to make good guesses. You will learn how to read new words.

Most important, the stories, poems, and articles are for you. Every person reading this book is different. So we picked many different stories. We want you to enjoy what you read.

Each reading has these four parts:

Before You Read

Here you will start thinking about the story. You will do things you should do every time you read.

You will also look at a few words that are important to the story. They are marked with a "word bank." You can use these words to make a word bank. You will learn how to make a word bank in Unit 1.

The Reading

This book has many readings. Some are fun or helpful. Some make you think.

In Unit 1, "People," you will read about some surprising people. Unit 2, "Coping," is about how people cope with different problems. In Unit 3, "Messages," you will hear from people with a message. And in Unit 4, "Cultures," you will learn about cultures around the world.

1

At the end of the book is a longer story. There are no questions with it. It is for you to enjoy and think about. That's what reading is about—learning and having fun.

Questions

After each reading are questions. The answers are in the back of the book.

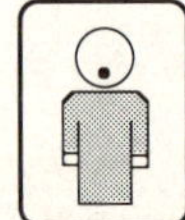 Some questions have a picture of a speaking person next to them. These are questions to talk about.

Other questions have lines to write on. Write as much as you can. Don't worry much about spelling. Just get your ideas down. If you can't write all your ideas, tell them to another person. That person can write them for you.

Think About It

This part asks what *you* think. It often asks you to write about your ideas first. Then it may ask you to talk about them with other people. Other people may have a different point of view. You learn more about what you think by talking with other people.

We hope you like your book. Happy reading!

1 People

The world is full of people. They are young and old, rich and poor, all shapes and sizes. Sometimes people do surprising things. Some people do great things. In this unit you will read about many different people. Some of them are well known. Others are not. All of them are surprising.

Using What You Know

You already know about many things. When you read, you learn new things. But to learn as you read, you have to use what you already know.

For example, the next story is about a man who saved people after an earthquake. What do you already know about earthquakes? Add your ideas to this *word map*. A word map is a way to order your ideas. Add as many ideas as you can think of. You can draw more circles if you want.

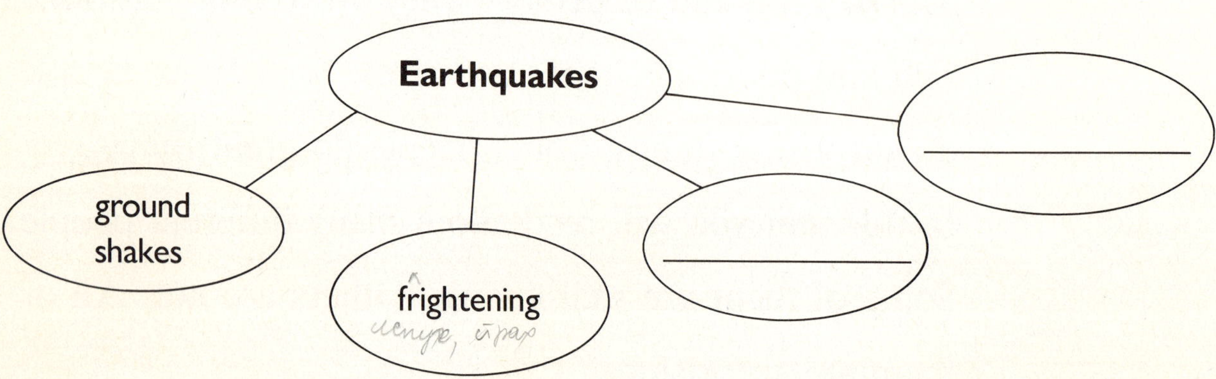

As you read the next story, think about what you know about earthquakes. It will help you understand the story.

Hints for Good Readers

- *Remember:* Use what you already know to help you learn more.

- Before you read something, look at the name of the story. Look at the pictures.

- Ask: What is this story about? What do I already know about this? What words will probably be used in this story?

People: "A Hero"

Before You Read

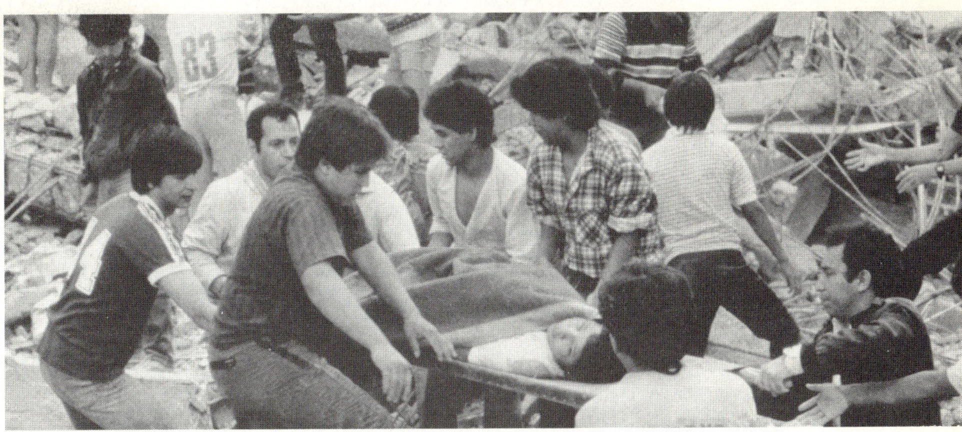

Rescue teams at work after 1985 earthquakes in Mexico City

Here are some words for your word bank. They are important in this story. "Words to Know" will always give you the meaning that each word has in the reading that follows. Read the words. Then guess what you think the story will be about.

Words to Know

hero   a person admired for courage or great deeds

rescue   to save from danger

Write both words in this sentence.

A _ _ _ _ _ will _ _ _ _ _ _ _ people from danger.

Say It Right

Some stories have names that are hard to say. You do not need to know how to say the name. Just keep reading. Here is how to say the name of the person in this story.

Marcos Efrén Zariñana   (MAR kohs   eh FREHN Zah ree NYA nah)

A Hero

What do you think a hero should be like? Should a hero be big? Strong? Should a hero be very smart? Should a hero have a loud voice that makes people stop and listen?

Marcos Efrén Zariñana is none of these. He is a thin and small man. He wears thick glasses. He speaks in a soft voice. In fact, as a boy, he was so little that people called him "*La Pulga.*" This is Spanish for "The Flea."

But Marcos will always be a hero to many people in his country, Mexico.

In the fall of 1985, very strong earthquakes hit Mexico City. As many as 30,000 people died. They were trapped under buildings that fell on them.

In the terrible days after the earthquakes, Marcos helped rescue people trapped under the buildings. He worked day and night, digging into the rubble. He almost never rested. Because he is so small, he could go where no one else fit.

Marcos had no training as a rescue worker. But he still rescued twenty-seven people. Some were almost dead when he got to them. He worked slowly and carefully, talking softly to them. He pulled them out to the doctors waiting for them.

The people were very grateful to Marcos. Stories about him were on the TV news for a long time after the earthquakes. Even the Mexican leaders honored him.

So what should heroes be like? They should be brave and kind. They should be people who never give up. They should be people who go where no one else can go.

They should be people like Marcos Efrén Zariñana.

Questions

1. Fill in the missing words. Use words from the box.

small   buildings   rescued
earthquakes   people

In 1985, Mexico City was hit by strong
__________ . Many people were killed when they
were trapped under __________ . Marcos Efrén
Zariñana helped rescue many __________ after
the earthquakes. Because he is __________ , he
could get under the fallen buildings. He
__________ twenty-seven people.

2. Write a few words to answer these questions. The first one is done for you.
   a. When Marcos was a boy, why did people call him "The Flea"?
   because he was small and thin

   b. After the 1985 earthquakes, what did Marcos do?

   c. How did his size help him?

3. Make up your own headline for this story. Here are some words you may want to use: *hero, rescue, The Flea, Mexico, earthquake.*

Think About It

brave   loud   kind   rich strong   smart   big

Which word in the box do you think is *most* important for a hero? Underline it.

Are there any words in the box that you think are *not* important for a hero? Cross them out.

Show your answers to someone else. Does that person agree with you about heroes? Talk about your answers with each other.

Do you know someone who seems like a hero? Write the person's name here.

____

Why do you think this person is a hero? Use a word from the box above.

____

Making Predictions Before You Read

Good readers make guesses before they read. They *predict*. They guess about what will be in the story.

A **prediction** is not just any guess. It is a good guess. Before they read, good readers look at the title or headline. They look at the pictures. Then they guess what the story is about.

Look at this picture and headline.

Workers On Strike For More Pay

You can tell a lot from the picture and words. Tell someone what you think the story will be about.

"But I may guess wrong," you say.

That's OK! A good guess can be wrong. And a wrong guess is better than no guess at all. Why? If you make a guess, you hold it in your mind as you read. You will think about the story. You will want to find out if you were right or wrong.

Even when you guess wrong, you will remember why your guess was wrong. More important, you will remember what the story was about. Look at the story on pages 12 and 13. Read the title of the story. Look at the picture on page 11. Make a guess.

I think Jaime Escalante
    a. teaches young children
    b. teaches high school
I think his students are
    a. rich
    b. poor

Hints for Good Readers

- Before you read something, look at the title. Look at the pictures.
- Guess what the story will be about.
- Read the story to see if your guess was right.

People: ''Jaime Escalante, Super Teacher''

Before You Read

Jaime Escalante in his classroom

Words to Know

cleaver   a big knife with a short handle, used for cutting meat

motivate   to make someone want to do something

Put the right word in each sentence.

a. A good teacher can _________ students.

b. You can cut meat with a _________ .

Say It Right

Jaime Escalante   (HY meh Ehs kah LAHN teh)

11

Jaime Escalante, Super Teacher

Stand and Deliver was a surprising hit movie in 1988. It told the story of a math teacher in a school in East L.A. Did you know that the story was true? The school is Garfield High School in East Los Angeles, California. Most of its students are poor and Hispanic. The math teacher is Jaime Escalante.

Escalante is always surprising his students. On his first day, his students had problems adding. They were counting on their fingers. Escalante didn't teach adding.

Instead, he brought in a meat cleaver. He put on a cook's hat. Waving the cleaver, he loudly cut an apple in two. "Let's talk about percentages," he said. No one else said a word.

That was 1974. Since then, Escalante has surprised hundreds of students. His students learn math. They do better than that. They take the advanced math test. The advanced math test for placing students in college is a very hard one. Only two percent of U.S. high school students take it. All of Escalante's students take it. About eighty percent of them pass the test.

Escalante makes his students work hard. He also has fun with them. And he makes them feel proud. "I tell them, 'You are the best. You are our hope for the future.'"

Escalante and his family came here from Bolivia in 1964. He had been a math teacher in Bolivia. But in the U.S., he couldn't teach with a Bolivian degree. So he worked in a coffee shop. He learned English. Then he got a better job. But he wanted to be a teacher. At night, he went to college so he could teach in the U.S.

Garfield High School has changed a lot since Escalante started teaching there in 1974. He and the other teachers have worked hard to make the school better. Now the gangs are gone. The drugs are gone. The building is clean. Garfield is a good school.

But there have been problems. In 1982, Escalante's students took the college math test. Fourteen of them made the same mistakes. This looked strange. They were accused of cheating. Escalante was angry. If they had not had Spanish names, he thought, they would never have been accused. All fourteen took a new, harder test. All passed.

Today, old Garfield students often drop by to see him. "Mr. Escalante's secret is he really cares," says Maria Torres, now in college. "I came back because I missed him."

Questions

1. Read these sentences about Jaime Escalante. If a sentence is true, circle the letter in front of it.
   a. He was born in East Los Angeles.
   b. He went to college so he could teach.
   c. He believes his students are the hope for the future.
   d. His students cheated on the college math test.
   e. *Stand and Deliver* was a movie about Escalante.

2. Jaime Escalante cut an apple in half with a cleaver. Why did he do that?
   a. He wanted to make class interesting so students would learn.
   b. He was hungry for an apple and didn't have a smaller knife.
   c. He was angry with the class.

Think About It

We meet many teachers in our lives. Not all our teachers are in school. Parents are teachers. Our friends can be teachers.

Think about one person in your life who has been a good teacher. Write down some ideas about this person.

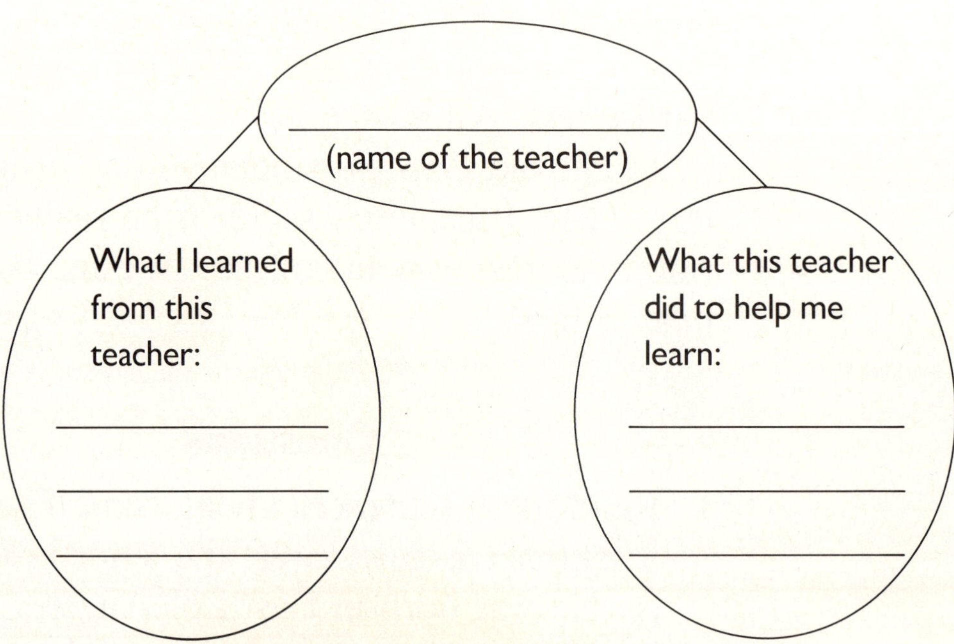

Now write a short letter to that person. Tell the person what you learned. Tell the person what he or she did to help you learn. If you want to, you can send your letter! Someone will be very happy to get it.

People: "Because"

Before You Read

Here is a poem by a well-known poet. Read the title and the poet's name. Then look at the first word in the poem. What is it? How do we usually write this word? ____

  Poems don't have to follow any rules. People who write poems make their own rules. When *you* write a poem, you can make your own rules too.

  Read the first four lines of the poem. Make a guess. What do you think this poem is about?

Read the poem to see if you are right.

Because   by Nikki Giovanni

i wrote a poem
for you because
you are
my little boy

i wrote a poem
for you because
you are
my darling daughter

and in this poem
i sang a song
that says
as time goes on
i am you
and you are me
and that's how life
goes on

About Nikki Giovanni

Yolande Cornelia Giovanni, Jr., was born in Tennessee in 1943. Later, she changed her name to Nikki Giovanni. She has written many books of poems. Her poems talk about feelings. Her poems talk about what it is like to be a black woman.

When you read a poem by Nikki Giovanni, be sure to read it out loud. Some of her poems sound like jazz or blues music. Some sound like gospel songs. Hearing her poems can be like listening to music.

Questions

1. Who is Nikki Giovanni talking to in the poem?
   a. her children
   b. her husband
   c. her mother

2. How does this poem make you feel?

____

____

____

Think About It

Nikki Giovanni's poem talks about the love between a parent and a child. What do you think she means by "i am you/and you are me/and that's how life/goes on"?

____

____

Try using part of Nikki Giovanni's poem to make up
your own poem. Write your poem to your children, or
a friend or loved one.

i am writing a poem
for you because

____

____

i am writing a poem
for you because

____

____

and in this poem

____

____

____

____

Reading a New Word

Reading is not just one thing. When you read a new word you are doing five things. Look at this sentence.

I buy bread at the grocery store.

If you understand the sentence, you have read it. The sentence tells you something. You read on.

But sometimes you don't know a word. What if you did not know the word *bread*? Here is what you can do.

1. Look at all the words you do know. Read them all. For the word you don't know, say "blank."

I buy *blank* at the grocery store.

2. This tells you the word is something you buy at the grocery store. But you can buy lots of things at a grocery store. How can you tell what it is?

3. You can look at the first letters of the word. They are *br.* What sound does *br* make? Read the sentence one more time. Use the *br* sound for the word.

I buy *br_* at the grocery store.

What thing in a grocery store begins with *br*? Often the word will now come to you—*bread*. You ask, "Does it make sense? Can you buy bread at the grocery store?" Yes, you can. *Bread* makes sense.

But what if the word still does not come to you?

With short words you can look at the last letters. The last letter is *d.* What sound does *d* make? Say the *br* with the *d.* "*Br___d.*" Read the sentence again and say "*br___d.*"

I buy *br___d* at the grocery store.

4. What thing in a grocery store sounds like *br___d*? Bread.

5. Try *bread* in the sentence. It makes sense.

Hints for Good Readers

How did you read the new word? You used five steps.

1. You read the words you knew. You said "blank" for the word you didn't know.

2. You thought about what words make sense in the sentence. You thought of things you can buy at grocery stores.

3. You looked at the beginning and ending sounds of the word.

4. You put steps 2 and 3 together and made a good guess.

5. You checked to see if your guess made sense.

All good readers use these five steps. Try them as you read this book.

Making a Word Bank

How do you remember new words? Here is one way that works for many people. Try making a **word bank.** When you find a word you want to remember, write the word on a card. On the back of the card, write a sentence using the word. This will help you remember what the word means. Keep the cards in a small box. Go over them often.

You can sort the cards into groups that go together. Here's an example. Look at these words.

fruit	chair	sofa	meat	TV
rug	eat	bed	popcorn	soda

Try writing each of the words in one of the two groups on page 20. After you use each word, draw a line through it.

Food Words
House Words

___________________   ___________________

___________________   ___________________

___________________   ___________________

___________________   ___________________

___________________   ___________________

You can also sort word bank words based on how the words are spelled and how they sound. For instance, two words in the list above have the letters *ea* in them. They are *meat* and *eat*. Can you think of any other words that have *ea* in them and sound like *meat* and *eat*? All these words could go in the same group.

Here's another way to sort words. Are any of the words in the box hard for you to spell? List them here.

Hard-to-Spell Words

____

____

____

How Does a Word Bank Help You?

Writing a word helps it to stay in your mind. Deciding what group to put the word in also helps you remember it. You can make groups of words you want to practice spelling. You can make groups of words you know and words you don't know.

Before each story are a few words. They are called "Words to Know." These are good words to add to your word bank. Add any other words you read that you want to remember. You can also add words you hear people say. You may want to add words you read in the paper or hear on the radio or TV. It is good to put any word you want to learn in a word bank.

People: "I Have a Dream"

Before You Read

Words to Know

creed   beliefs

character   the personality or moral qualities of a person

exalted   raised up

straight   without a bend or curve

A Reading Tip What is hard about the word *straight?* The letters *aigh* are not said the way you might expect. They make the same *a* sound as in *ate.*

This is a speech. Martin Luther King, Jr., gave the speech on August 28, 1963, in Washington, D.C. More than 200,000 people heard him. Most of them were black Americans. They had come together to show they wanted to be free. There are many ways to be free.

- free to live where you want
- free to say what you think
- free from someone's control

Can you think of other freedoms?

- free to _______________________________
- free from _____________________________

As you read the speech, try to hear it in your mind.

I Have a Dream by Martin Luther King, Jr.

I say to you today, my friends,
even though we face the difficulties
of today and tomorrow, I still have a dream.

It is a dream deeply rooted in the American dream.

I have a dream that one day this nation will rise up
and live out the true meaning of its creed:
"We hold these truths to be self-evident,
that all men are created equal.". . .

I have a dream that my four little children
will one day live in a nation where
they will not be judged by the color of their skin,
but by the content of their character.

I have a dream today! . . .

I have a dream that one day
"Every valley shall be exalted
and every hill and mountain shall be made low.

The rough places will be made plain*
and the crooked places will be made straight
and the glory of the Lord shall be revealed,
and all flesh shall see it together."

This is our hope.

This is the faith that I go back to the South with. . . .

*In this case, *plain* means flat.

With this faith
    we will be able to work together,
    to pray together,
    to struggle together,
    to go to jail together,
    to stand up for freedom together
    knowing that we will be free one day.

And this will be the day.
This will be the day
    when all of God's children
    will be able to sing with new meaning:
    "My country 'tis of thee
    sweet land of liberty
    of thee I sing.
    Land where my fathers died
    land of the pilgrim's pride
    from every mountainside, let freedom ring."

And if America is to be a great nation,
    this must become true.

So let freedom ring
    from the . . . hilltops of New Hampshire;
    let freedom ring
    from the mighty mountains of New York;
    let freedom ring
    from the heightening Alleghenies of Pennsylvania;
    let freedom ring
    from the snow-capped Rockies of Colorado;
    let freedom ring
    from the . . . slopes of California.
But not only that.

Let freedom ring
      from Stone Mountain of Georgia;
      let freedom ring
      from Lookout Mountain of Tennessee;
      let freedom ring
      from every hill and molehill of Mississippi.

From every mountainside, let freedom ring.

And when this happens
      and when we allow freedom to ring,
      when we let it ring from every village
      and every hamlet,
      from every state and every city,
      we will be able to speed up that day
      when all God's children,
      black men and white men,
      Jews and Gentiles,
      Protestants and Catholics,
      will be able to join hands and sing
      in the words of the old Negro spiritual:

"Free at last. Free at last.

Thank God Almighty,

We are free at last."

About Martin Luther King, Jr.

Martin Luther King, Jr., was born in Atlanta,
Georgia, in 1929. In the 1950s and 1960s he worked
very hard for civil rights. At that time, many laws kept
black people from voting, living where they wanted to,
and getting good jobs. He worked to change those
laws. In 1964, he received the Nobel Peace Prize for
his work.

But not everyone liked what King had to say. In 1968, he was shot and killed. Now he is remembered as a hero in the civil rights movement.

Questions

1. In his speech, Martin Luther King, Jr., says many times, "Let freedom ring." This means:
   a. Let everyone have a job.
   b. Let all people have free food and clothing.
   c. Let us hear that all people are free.

2. What does King dream for his own four children?
   a. that they will be judged by the color of their skin
   b. that they will be judged for the kind of people they are
   c. that they will not be judged

3. Many years have passed since Martin Luther King, Jr., fought and died for freedom. Do you think all people in the United States have freedom now? Talk about your ideas with someone.

Think About It

Martin Luther King had a dream of freedom for all people. What are some of your dreams for all people? Make a list and share it with someone else.

My Dreams for All People

1. ____

2. ____

3. ____

4. ____

5. ____

People:
"Martin Luther King" and
"Lincoln Monument: Washington"

Before You Read

Words to Know

overcome   to win

timeless   never ending

What two little words make up each of these big words?

overcome = ___________ + ___________

timeless = ___________ + ___________

A Reading Tip If you have trouble reading a long word, look for smaller words in it.

The next two poems talk about two great American leaders, Martin Luther King and Abraham Lincoln.

Abraham Lincoln lived 100 years before Martin Luther King. But the two men were alike in some ways. Both worked hard for the rights of black people. While he was President, Abraham Lincoln ended slavery in the United States. Like Martin Luther King, he wanted all people to be free.

The world was shocked when President Lincoln was killed by a gunman in 1865. Today the Lincoln Memorial in Washington, D.C., reminds us of "Old Abe."

Martin Luther King

by Myra Cohn Livingston

Got me a special place
For Martin Luther King.
His picture on the wall
Makes me sing.

I look at it for a long time
And think of some
Real good ways
We will overcome.

Lincoln Monument: Washington

by Langston Hughes

Let's go see old Abe
Sitting in the marble and the moonlight,
Sitting lonely in the marble and the moonlight,
Quiet for ten thousand centuries, old Abe.
Quiet for a million, million years.

Quiet—

And yet a voice forever
Against the
Timeless walls
Of time—
Old Abe.

Questions

1. Look at the first poem. How does the poet feel about Martin Luther King?

   ____

   ____

2. The poet has a picture of Martin Luther King on her wall. Do you have any pictures on your walls at home? Tell someone about one of them.

3. People in the civil rights movement say "We shall overcome" when they think of all the problems they still have to solve. When the author says she thinks "of some/Real good ways/We will overcome," what do you think she means?

4. Look at the second poem. When the author says, "Let's go see old Abe," what does he go see?
   a. Abraham Lincoln
   b. a statue of Abraham Lincoln
   c. Abraham Lincoln's family

5. The poem says old Abe is quiet. But the poem also says that he is "a voice forever." What do you think this means?

   ____

   ____

   ____

6. Look at each sentence below. Write "AL" if the sentence is true about Abraham Lincoln. Write "MLK" if it is true about Martin Luther King, Jr. Write "Both" if the sentence is true about both of them.

_____ a. He lived more than 100 years ago.

_____ b. He believed all people should be free.

_____ c. He was shot and killed.

_____ d. He was President of the United States.

Think About It

Which of these two poems do you like best?

____

How do you feel when you read it?

____

____

____

Read the poem to someone else. Ask that person to tell you how the poem makes him or her feel.

People: "Grandma Moses"

Before You Read

Words to Know

astonished   very surprised

solution   answer to a problem

Put the right word in each sentence.

1. We need a __________ to the problem of drugs.

2. Grandma Moses was __________ when a man bought her paintings.

A Reading Tip Look at the last part of the word *solution*. The letters *tion* make a *shun* sound. Underline the letters that make the *shun* sound in these words.

nation	station	recreation
question	digestion	tradition

You are going to read about a famous painter. Think of a few words that go with the idea of painting. Add them to the map.

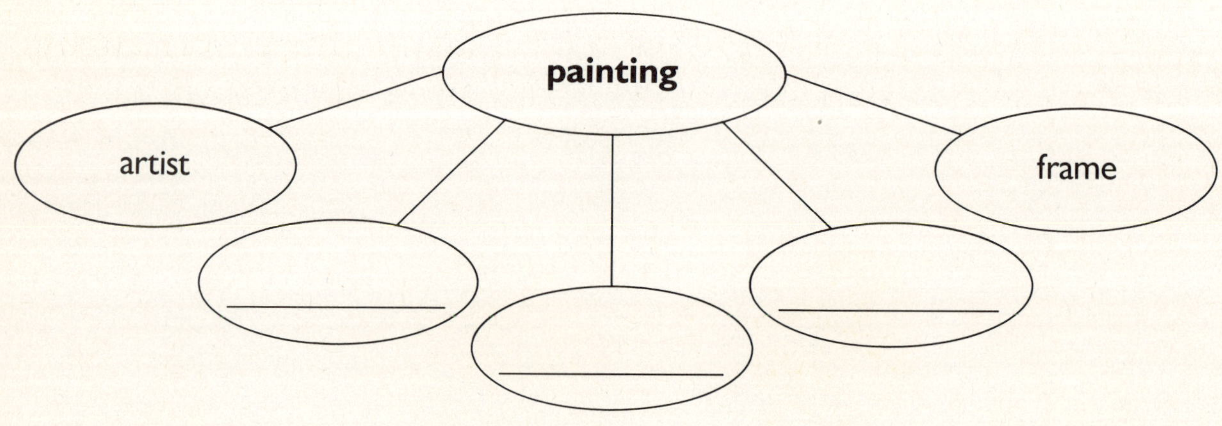

Grandma Moses

Grandma Moses. That's what people liked to call her. She was Anna Mary Robertson Moses. Born in 1860, she died in 1961. She was in her seventies when she began to paint. She lived on farms all her life. So that's what she painted. People loved her pictures of country life. By the time she died, she was famous. Zibby Oneal's book Grandma Moses *is based on Grandma Moses' autobiography* My Life's History. *In her book, Zibby Oneal tells of the day Grandma Moses sold her first paintings.*

On that day, a man from New York City named Louis J. Caldor was passing through Hoosick Falls. He happened to glance in the drugstore window, and he liked the paintings he saw there. He went into the store to ask about them. When he came out, he had the paintings under his arm and Grandma Moses' address in his pocket. He wanted to buy more.

When Grandma Moses heard this, she was astonished. He'd bought those pictures and he wanted more! How many more did he want? she wondered. Someone had told him that there might be as many more as ten.

Grandma Moses spent a sleepless night. She was trying to remember where other pictures might be. She didn't think there *were* ten more pictures. Maybe, together with her worsted* pictures, there were almost enough. But ten? Toward morning, she thought of a

*made of yarn

solution. There was a painting—quite a large one—she remembered. If she could find a couple of frames in the morning, she could saw the picture in half and have two.

She did just that. When Mr. Caldor arrived, she had ten pictures to show him.

The Old Oaken Bucket, a painting by Grandma Moses

Questions

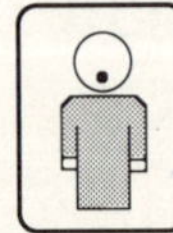

1. Look at the painting above. Tell someone what you see in it.

2. Why did Louis J. Caldor want to buy Grandma Moses' paintings?

____

____

3. Grandma Moses could not fall asleep. Why couldn't she sleep?

    a. She did not want to sell her paintings.

    b. She did not like Mr. Caldor.

    c. She could not remember where her paintings were.

4. Fill in the missing words. Use the words in the box.

sell	buy	ten	country
paint	cut	paintings	

Grandma Moses liked to __________ . She painted pictures of __________ life. One day, Louis J. Caldor saw her __________ in a store. He wanted to __________ ten of them. Grandma Moses did not have __________ paintings. She __________ a big painting in half. Then she had ten paintings to __________ to Mr. Caldor.

Think About It

Grandma Moses began to paint when she was in her seventies. She was not afraid to learn something new. What are some things you would like to learn to do? Make a list. Then share your list with someone else.

Things I Would Like to Learn

1. ____________________

2. ____________________

3. ____________________

4. ____________________

Looking Back

Word Bank

By now you should have ten to fifteen words in your word bank. Your word bank probably has the "Words to Know" from each reading. You may also have cards for other words that you want to remember.

Look over all the words you have in your word bank. What groups can you put them in? Make a group of words that you have trouble spelling. Practice copying these words. Then try to write them without looking at the words. When you learn a word, take it out of the "Hard-to-Spell" group.

Perhaps you have some words that describe people. This is another way to sort your words. You can also try putting all your words in order from A to Z. In this case, *astonished* might be the first word in your group.

Writing

Choose one of the people you have read about in this unit. Write a few words on the map to tell about that person.

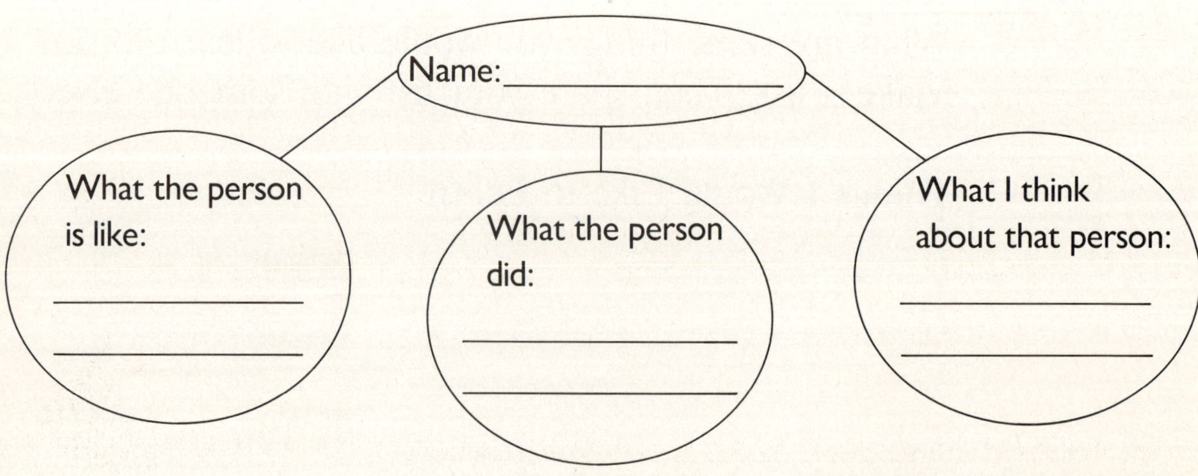

Coping

Life keeps changing! Sometimes changes are good. Sometimes they are bad. Sometimes it's hard to cope with everything that happens. It can be hard to decide what to do.

But we can learn ways to handle our problems. We can learn how to cope. In this unit you will read about ways to cope with different kinds of problems. As you read, ask yourself: How would I cope with this problem?

Learning New Words

If you cannot read a word, or if you do not know what it means, keep reading. The words and sentences that come after the word may help you.

1. If a word is unusual, the writer may try to help the reader. Sometimes the writer will tell you what the word means right after it.

What does the underlined word mean in these sentences?

> The first runner took the lead in the race. She passed the <u>baton</u>, or stick, to the second runner.

A baton is a _______ used in a race.

2. Often you can guess a hard word by reading the next sentence. Remember to read past the word you do not know.

Look for the meaning of the underlined word in the sentence that comes after it.

> This coat has a spot on it. Can you give me a <u>discount</u>? Can I pay a little less for it?

You can tell a discount means
- **a.** to pay more
- **b.** to pay less
- **c.** a new coat

3. Sometimes you need to read several sentences. Then you can make a good guess about a hard word. See if you can guess the underlined word by reading all of these sentences.

> <u>Tension.</u> All people feel it. Too much tension can harm the body. The heart pounds. Breathing is fast. Muscles get tight. When this happens, it is important to relax.

The sentences tell you all these things about the word *tension*.

- It is a feeling.
- It is bad for you.
- It makes your heart pound and your muscles tight.

Circle the sentences on page 36 that tell you these things.

Now make a guess about *tension*. *Tension* probably means

    a. feeling happy and relaxed
    b. feeling unhappy and tight

A Reading Tip You can think about the sound of a word too. What is the first sound in the word *tension?* What sound does *sion* make?

Remember Add the words called "Words to Know" to your word bank. Also add new or hard words you read or hear.

Coping: "How to Save Money"

Before You Read

Words to Know

coupon   (KOO pahn *or* KYOO pahn) a small piece of paper that gives a person money off the price

discount   the amount taken off a price

This reading is about how to save money. What are some ways you already know to save money? List them here.

Ways to Save Money

1. ____

2. ____

3. ____

4. ____

Now read to find out some more ways to save money.

How to Save Money

Here are some tips for saving money. Most likely you already do some of these things. Others may be new ideas. Try them!

Get the Best Price You Can

- Cut coupons from the paper.

- Look for sales.

- When your brand of coffee is on sale, buy several cans. The same goes for anything you buy all the time.

- Make deals. Say, "This coat has a spot. Can I get a discount? Can you give it to me for less?"

- If you are over 55, ask about discounts for older people. You can get them on food, movies, and buses.

- Shop at discount stores. Look for yard sales. Buy work clothes, baby clothes, books, furniture, and kitchen things at second-hand stores.

- Buy things at the end of the season. Air conditioners go on sale in the fall. Snow shovels are less in April.

- Read consumer magazines. These magazines tell you the best buys on everything from cars to soap. Talk to people. Find out what brands are good.

Form Money-Saving Habits

- Take care of your car. Change the oil every three months. Put air in the tires. Paint rust spots right away. Your car will hold up longer.

- Go to the early showing of a movie. You often pay less.

- Check out free ways to have fun. Go to summer fairs and free concerts. Have a picnic in the park.

- Make long-distance calls at night or on weekends. The rates are lower.

- Try to pay off your credit card each month. That way you don't have to pay interest.

- Take a bag lunch to work. Bring coffee or tea from home in a thermos.

- Don't use prepared foods. You pay more for frozen and canned dinners than home-cooked ones.

Questions

1. You go to the store to buy a bar of soap. You see the soap you like is on sale. What is the best thing to do to save money?
   a. Don't buy any soap.
   b. Buy just one bar of soap.
   c. Buy a few extra bars of soap for later.

2. Which of these things would NOT save you money?
   a. saving coupons
   b. reading *Consumer Reports*
   c. buying frozen dinners

3. Why would air conditioners go on sale in the fall?

   ____

   ____

4. What are some fun things you can do for free?

5. List three ways to save money on food.

   a. ____________________________

   b. ____________________________

   c. ____________________________

Think About It

You have read about many ways to save money. Ask some friends how they save money. Do they have any new ideas? If they do, list them here.

   1. ____________________________

   2. ____________________________

   3. ____________________________

Tell your friends what you learned about saving money.

Finding the Main Idea

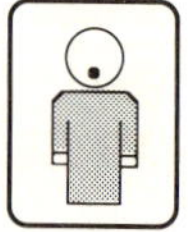

You want to see a show on TV. You look at the listing in the paper. One show sounds good. The paper tells a little about it. It says the show tells how one town is fighting back against drugs. The paper has told you the **main idea** of the show.

Try this with a friend now. Pick a TV show you have seen in the last day or two. Think about it for a minute. See if you can tell the main idea to your friend in five seconds or less.

Finding the main idea is important when you read. But you do not tell it to a friend. You tell the main idea to yourself.

Two Ways the Main Idea Helps You Read

1. It helps you understand what you read.
As you read, ask, "What is this about?" If you are not sure, stop and think. Sometimes you may need to go back and read again.

When you finish reading, stop again. Try to say what the story was about in one or two sentences.

2. It helps you remember what you read.
The main idea is like a coatrack. You can hang details of the story on it. Details are the smaller parts of a story. They can be people, or places, or things. The most important details are the smaller ideas that make up the main idea.

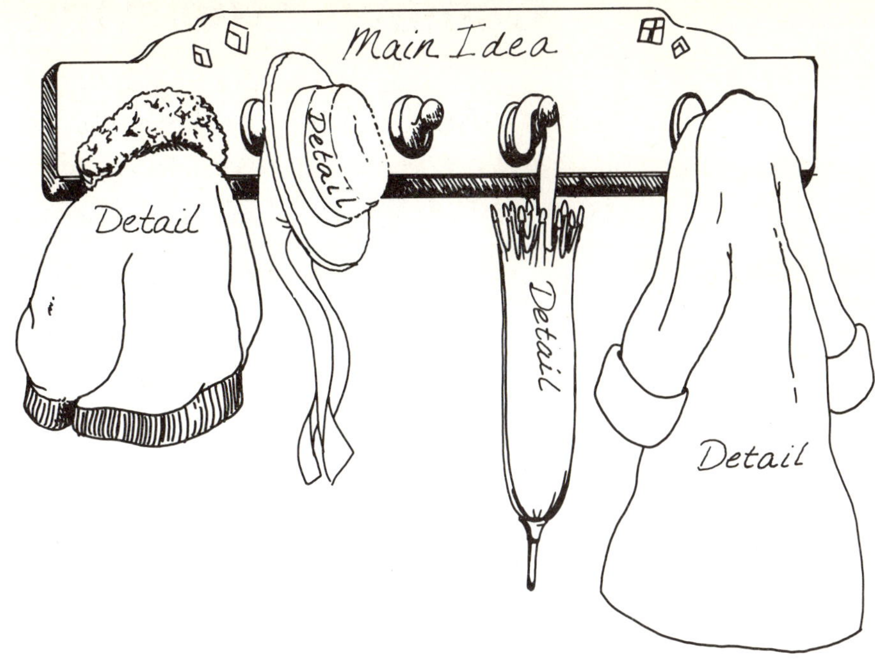

If you hang your coat on a coatrack, it will be easier to find. If you "hang" the details you read about on a main idea, they will be easier to remember.

Hints for Good Readers

- When you read, ask, "What is this about?" Try to say the main idea in one or two sentences.

- Think of a few important details. Hang them on the main idea. You will remember them better.

Coping: "Jim Abbott"

Before You Read

Jim Abbott

Words to Know

rookie   a beginner

field   in baseball, to stop or catch a ball after it is
hit by a bat

Add these words to your word bank. You might want
to start a group of sports words.

Look at the name of this story. Look at the picture.
Who is this story about?

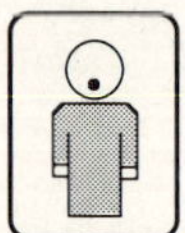

Do you know anything about Jim Abbott? If you
do, tell what you know.

As you read, look for the most important idea in
each paragraph. It is written in the margin. Fill in the
missing letters.

Jim Abbott, Rookie on the Rise

He's just a rookie. But all eyes are on this California Angels' pitcher. For one thing, Jim Abbott is a great athlete.

He's young, just 21. He's strong. At six foot three, 200 pounds, he throws 94 miles an hour.

In high school, he played football. He quarterbacked. At the University of Michigan, it was baseball. He pitched. He pitched very well. In 1987, he got the Sullivan Award. It is given to the best U.S. amateur athlete.

Then came the 1988 Olympics. Abbott's pitching helped the U.S. team to win the gold medal.

Abbott was the Angels' first pick in 1989. No one was surprised.

But there is another reason for the attention. Jim Abbott was born without a right hand. It's easy to see that it didn't hold him back. His parents never made him feel different. They brought him up like any other boy. "I just did things," says Abbott.

American League pitchers don't have to bat. But they do have to field. Abbott holds a glove on his right arm. He throws. Then he slips the glove on to his left hand. It's done so quickly that one hardly notices.

Abbott says he always dreamed of playing baseball. But, he says, "I can't remember how many hands I had in my dreams."

Questions

Fill in the blanks to tell the main idea about the story on page 45.

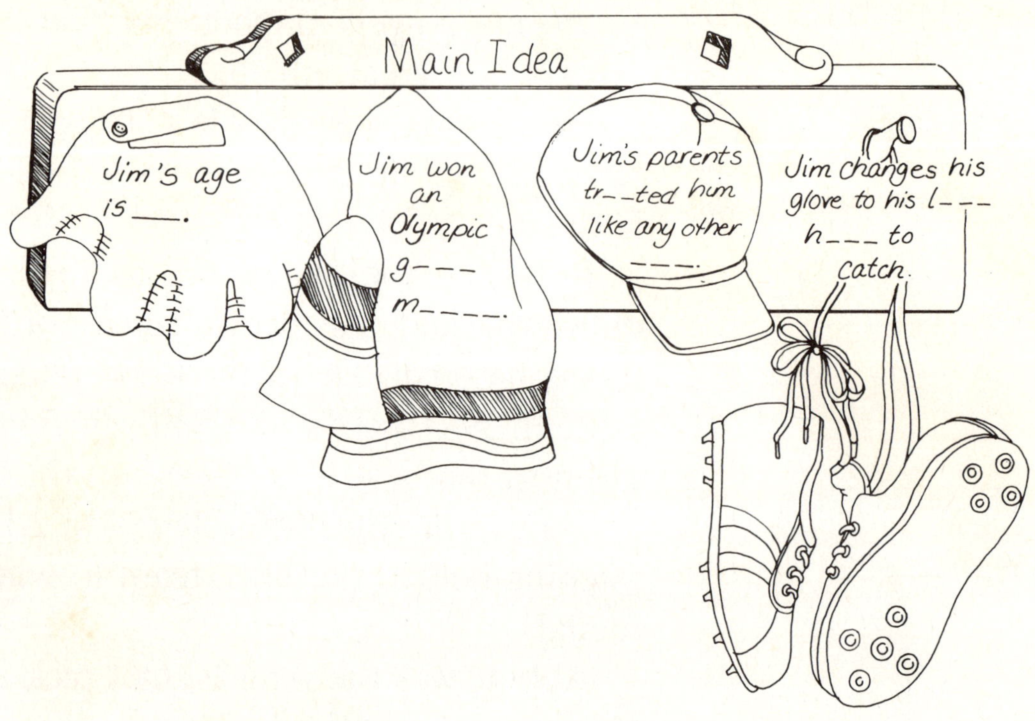

Think About It

Who would think a man with one hand could play baseball? Many people would say it was impossible. But Jim Abbott was not afraid to try.

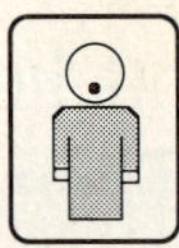

Why wasn't Jim Abbott afraid to try? Share your ideas with someone else.

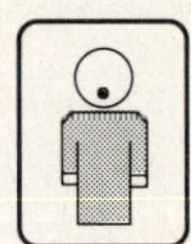

Do you know anyone who has overcome a handicap? Tell about that person.

Coping: "Dream Variation"

Before You Read

What is the title of this poem?

____

What do you think of when you hear the word *dream*? Write down all the words you think of. Add them to this word map. You can put in more circles.

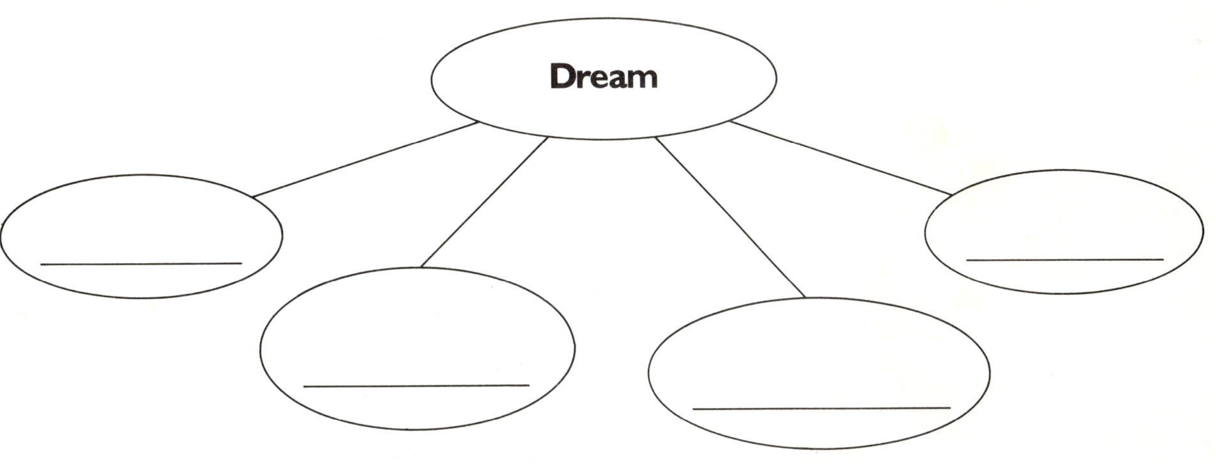

Words to Know

fling   to throw wildly

whirl   to spin fast

gently   softly, quietly

tenderly   lovingly

These four words are important in the poem on the next page. The words *fling* and *whirl* are very different from the words *gently* and *tenderly*.

There are two different moods in the poem. One mood is active and lively. The other mood is quiet and calm. Look for these moods as you read the poem.

Read the poem at the bottom of the page.

Write any words from the poem here that show movement and action.

____

Write any words from the poem here that show quiet and calm.

____

People can have different parts to their dreams. They can also be in different moods. What words would you use to tell about your moods?

____

Dream Variation by Langston Hughes

To fling my arms wide
In some place of the sun,
To whirl and to dance
Till the white day is done.
Then rest at cool evening
Beneath a tall tree
While night comes on gently,
  Dark like me—
That is my dream!

To fling my arms wide
In the face of the sun,
Dance! Whirl! Whirl!
Till the quick day is done.
Rest at pale evening . . .
A tall, slim tree . . .
Night coming tenderly
  Black like me.

Questions

1. How are the poet and the night alike?

   ____

2. How does this poem make you feel?

   ____

3. How do you think Langston Hughes felt when
   he wrote it?

   ____

4. The poet tells his dreams about what life could
   be. What do you think his life is *really* like? Tell
   someone your ideas.

Think About It

Langston Hughes has written a poem that tells his
dreams. What are your dreams? Write a few words on
the map about them.

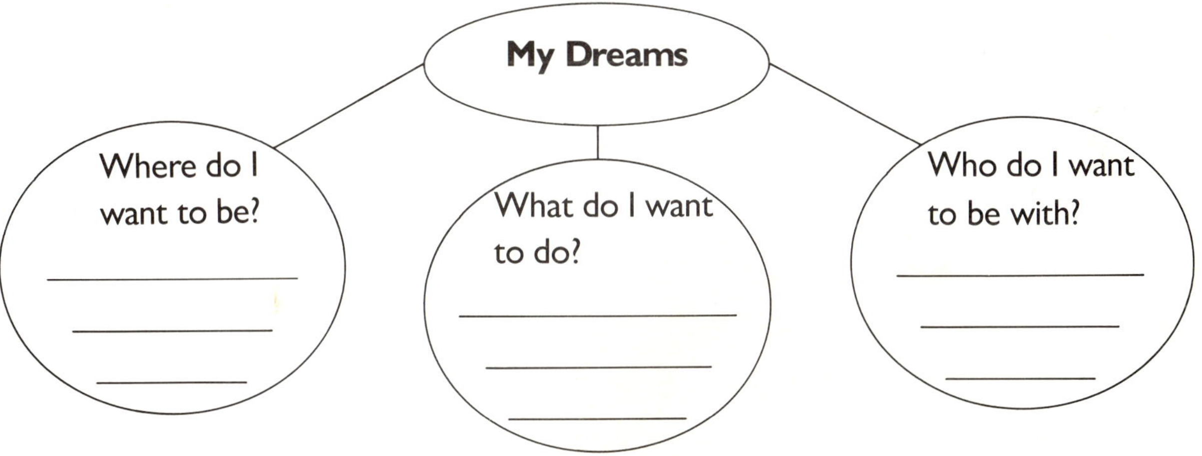

Can you write a poem about your dreams?
Remember, your words don't have to rhyme. When
you write a poem, you can make your own rules.

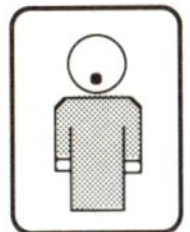
Write your poem on your own paper. Think of a
name for it. If you want, share your poem with
someone else.

Coping: "How Much Is Smoking Hurting You?"

Before You Read

You will be taking a quiz about smoking. What do you already know about smoking? Write your ideas on the map.

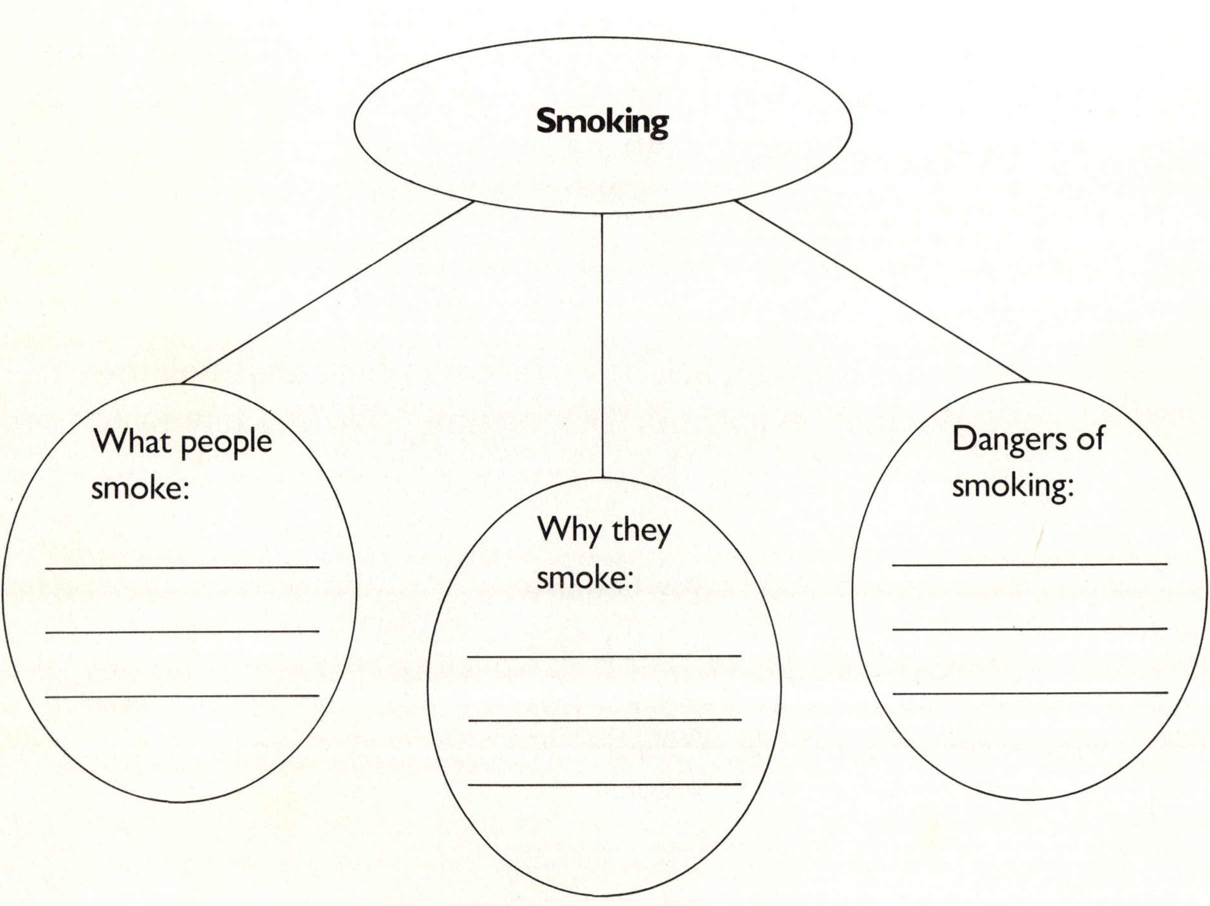

How Much Is Smoking Hurting You?

All smoking hurts you. How much it hurts you
depends on several things. Answer each of the following questions. Each time you answer YES, add up the
points. This will give you an idea of just how much
your smoking is hurting *you*.

If you don't smoke, try to answer for someone who
does. Think of a friend or a relative who smokes. If
you want, ask someone the questions and write down
the answers.

1. Do you smoke a pipe? 2 points

2. Do you smoke:
    a. 1 to 4 cigars a day? 2 points
    b. 5 to 10 cigars a day? 4 points
    c. more than 10 cigars a day? 7 points

3. Do you smoke:
    a. 1 to 9 cigarettes a day? 10 points
    b. 10 to 19 cigarettes a day? 15 points
    c. 20 to 39 cigarettes a day? 18 points
    d. more than 39 cigarettes a day? 24 points

4. Have you smoked for:
    a. less than 15 years? 2 points
    b. 15 to 25 years? 7 points
    c. 26 to 35 years? 9 points
    d. more than 35 years? 13 points

5. If you smoke cigarettes, are they "high tar" ones?
   4 points

6. Do you smoke your cigar or cigarette down to the
   butt? 7 points

7. Do you usually take the smoke into your lungs? 10
   points

If your points add up to:

- less than 10—You have little need to worry.
- between 10 and 25—Your chances for a long and healthy life are in danger.
- more than 25—Your life and health are in great danger.

No matter how much you smoke, you should stop. Your chances of getting sick from smoking go down from the moment you stop.

Questions

1. What does the quiz tell you?
   a. how many cigarettes you smoke
   b. how long you have been smoking
   c. how much smoking is hurting you

2. How many points do you get if you smoke five cigarettes a day? _______________________

3. Is it safe to smoke five cigarettes a day? Explain.

____

____

4. The person who wrote this quiz believes
   a. People should only smoke cigars.
   b. People should not smoke at all.
   c. People should take the smoke into their lungs.

5. Read the following sentences. Write "T" if a sentence is true. Write "F" if a sentence is false.

   _______ a. The longer you smoke, the more smoking hurts you.

   _______ b. Even if you quit smoking, your health will not get better.

   _______ c. It is better for your health to smoke "high tar" cigarettes.

   _______ d. Smoking a pipe is better than smoking cigarettes.

Think About It

More and more places have "No Smoking" signs. People who don't smoke say they want clean air. But smokers say they have no place to smoke any more. What do you think? Where should people be able to smoke? Where should people NOT be able to smoke? Share your ideas with someone else.

Make a list of the places you think of.

OK Places To Smoke	**"No Smoking" Places**
1. ___________________	1. ___________________
2. ___________________	2. ___________________
3. ___________________	3. ___________________

Picturing What You Read

Karen has just seen a movie. Matt asks her how she liked it. "I was so scared," says Karen. "I felt like I was right there!"

Good readers feel like they are "right there" when they read. They get a good picture of what is happening in the story. They think about what they would see, hear, smell, taste, or touch. They look for details that help them picture the story better.

As you read the next story, try to see it in your mind. Think about what the people look like. Think about what their house looks like. Think about the sounds they hear. Think about how the people feel. For extra help, use the questions on the side.

Hints for Good Readers

- When you read, try to picture what is happening.

- Look for words that tell what you would see, hear, smell, taste, or touch.

- The more you can picture the story, the more you will understand it.

Coping: ''Sleep, Baby, Sleep''

Before You Read

Words to Know

couple   two people

fault   something to be blamed for

Look at the title of the story. Look at the picture.
What do you think the story will be about?

I think the story will be about _______________

____ .

"Asleep," the young mother said to her husband. She was talking about their baby.

"Thank goodness," he said. He was glad to hear such good news. He thought his son would never go to sleep. He was very tired. So was his wife. Their little baby woke up crying all the time. They had no idea what to do.

"I stroked his hair until he finally closed his eyes," the wife said.

"Don't spoil him," the husband said. "People at work say that. It is not good to let him push us around."

"But maybe he felt sick. Or maybe he had a bad dream. Poor little guy! I couldn't just let him cry!" the wife said.

"I hope we did the right thing," the husband said.

"I hope he sleeps until morning," the wife said.

The young couple went back to bed. They both quickly fell asleep. An hour later, they heard the baby crying again.

"Do you think we should give him a bottle?" the wife asked. "Maybe he wants milk."

"No. No bottles. He's too old to still be having night feedings. I think he just wants to see us. I'll go check in with him."

The husband looked at his son crying. What was it? Why didn't the baby just sleep through the night? Other babies did it. He wondered what to do. He felt so tired. He was even a little angry at his baby.

What do you picture here?

What would the baby sound like? How would his parents look now?

Where is the husband now? How would he look?

Then he thought about it. It was not his
baby's fault. He just woke up crying. It was no
one's fault. It just happened. He didn't know
why. He didn't know what to do. The only
thing he knew was that he loved his new little
family.

He put his hand softly on his son's back
and talked to him. The baby stopped crying.
For this time tonight, the father had his
answers.

Questions

1. How do the young parents feel?
   a. tired
   b. angry at each other
   c. happy

2. Why don't they give the baby a bottle?
   a. They think a bottle will make him cry.
   b. They think he is too old for night feedings.
   c. They do not have any milk to give him.

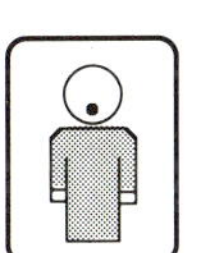

3. Why does the husband go to see the baby?

4. Why is the husband a little angry at the baby?

5. Does the husband stay angry? Explain.

Think About It

Everyone has different ideas about crying babies.
Some people pick them up. Some people let them cry.
What do you think? Write your ideas below.

When a baby cries, you should ___________________

____ .

This is because ___________________________________

____ .

Coping: "Miracle in Rome"

Before You Read

Words to Know

miracle   a wonderful thing that happens

baton   (ba TAHN) a light stick

Say It Right

Olympics   (oh LIM piks)—This sports contest happens every four years in a different country. Teams from all over the world compete in many different sports.

This story is about the 1960 Olympics. How many years ago was the 1960 Olympics held? _____ What do you already know about the Olympics? Add it to the map.

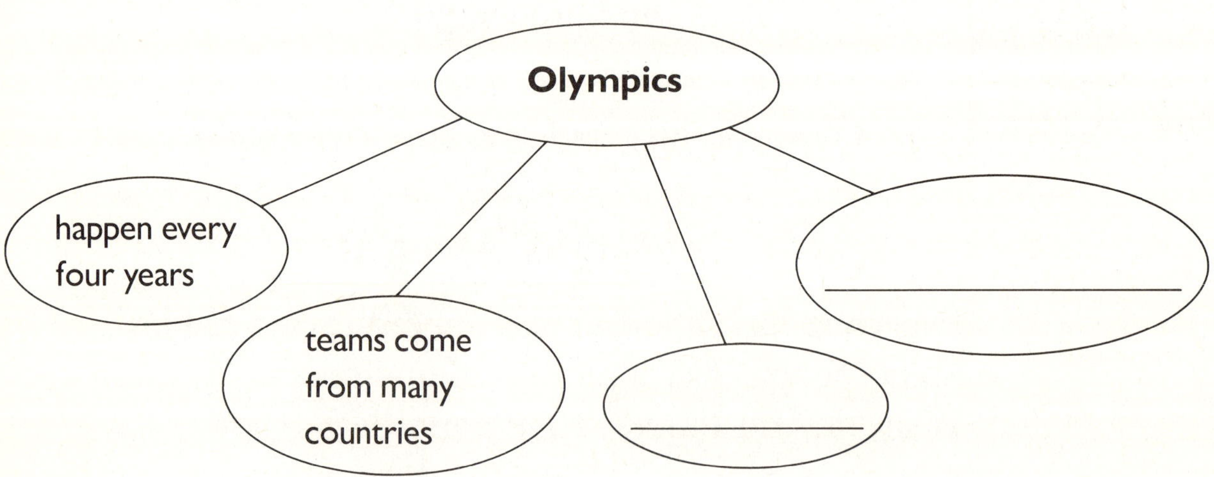

As you read, pretend you are at the 1960 Olympics. What do you see?

Miracle in Rome by Betty Millsaps Jones

On September 8, 1960, Wilma Rudolph stood in the Olympic Stadium in Rome, Italy. She had come to run. For Wilma, it was like a miracle. As a child, she had not even been able to walk.

When Wilma was four, she was very sick. First she had scarlet fever. Then she got pneumonia. Doctors saved her. But she could not move her left leg. The doctors said she might never walk again. Her mother said, "Wilma *will* walk again."

One day each week, Wilma and her mother got up early. They rode a bus to the hospital. It was a long, hard trip.

Slowly, Wilma's leg got stronger. When she was six she wore a brace. Two years later, the doctors took the brace off. Wilma limped. But she could walk! For three more years, she wore special shoes. She had not been able to run and play before. Now she wanted to run everywhere.

Wilma Rudolph at start of race

Nine years later Wilma was in the 1960 Olympics. She had won two gold medals in two races. On September 8, she could win a third. Wilma and three other Americans would run the relay race.

The starting gun fired. The first American runner jumped out fast and took the lead. She passed the baton. The second American raced down the track. She passed the baton too. The third runner held the lead. She ran toward Wilma, holding out the baton.

The crowd gasped. The third runner had nearly dropped the baton! A runner from Germany raced past Wilma!

Wilma took the baton and ran.

Years before, Wilma's mother had told her, "Never give up. Never give up." Wilma remembered.

She closed on the German runner. Near the finish line, Wilma leaned forward. The crowd roared. Wilma Rudolph had won her third gold medal.

Wilma Rudolph crossing finish line at 1960 Olympics

Questions

1. Doctors thought Wilma would never walk again.
   Why did they think this?
   a. She had broken her leg.
   b. She had been sick.
   c. She was born with bad legs.

2. Write 1, 2, 3, and 4 to show what happened
   first, second, third, and fourth.

   _____ a. Wilma had scarlet fever.

   _____ b. She wore special shoes.

   _____ c. She went to Rome.

   _____ d. She wore a brace.

3. At the end of the relay race, what happened?
   a. The German runner won.
   b. Wilma dropped the baton.
   c. Wilma won the race.

4. Why was it a miracle that Wilma was at the
   Olympics?

   ____

   ____

Think About It

How can sports change a person's life? Think of one
person whose life has been changed by sports. Share
your ideas with someone else.

Coping: "Relax with Exercise"

Before You Read

Words to Know

tension a strain

shoulders the top of the back where the arms join the neck

muscles body parts that move the body

Read these three words. They are important words in this reading. Look at the title of the reading. Look at the pictures. What do you think this reading will be about?

____

____

____

What would you like to learn from this reading?

____

____

____

Relax with Exercise

Tension. All people feel it sometimes. But too much tension can harm the body. The heart pounds. Breathing is heavy and fast. Muscles become tight. When this happens, it is important to relax. One way to relax is through exercise. The following exercises can be done in a very short time.

1. Make sure the room is warm. Your clothes should be comfortable, not tight. Lie down on your back. Close your eyes.

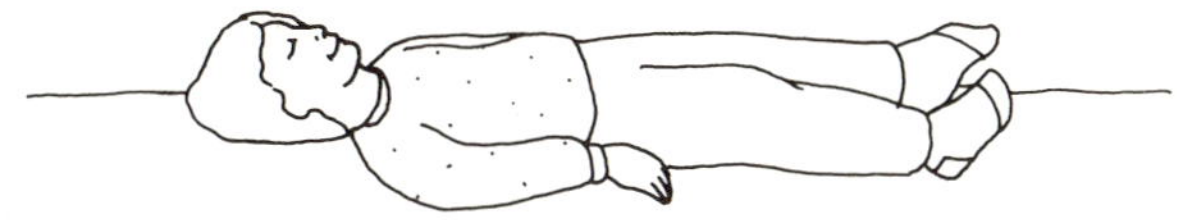

2. Make the muscles of your face tight. Then relax them.

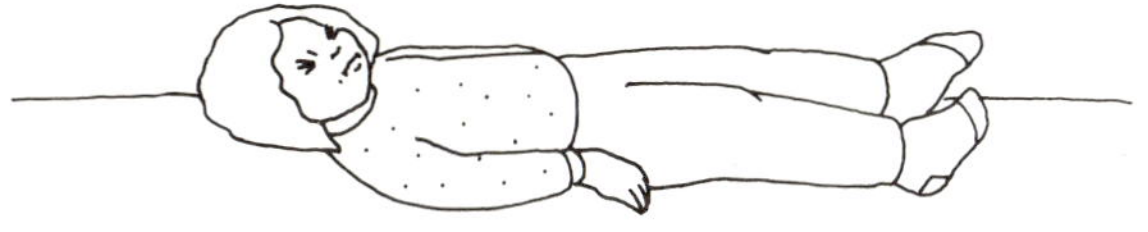

3. Lift your head off the floor. Let it fall softly back. Keep your face and neck relaxed.

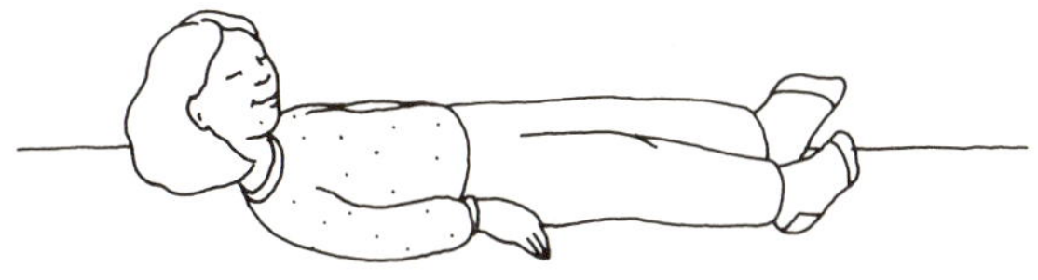

4. Push your shoulders against the floor. Hold for a moment. Then relax.

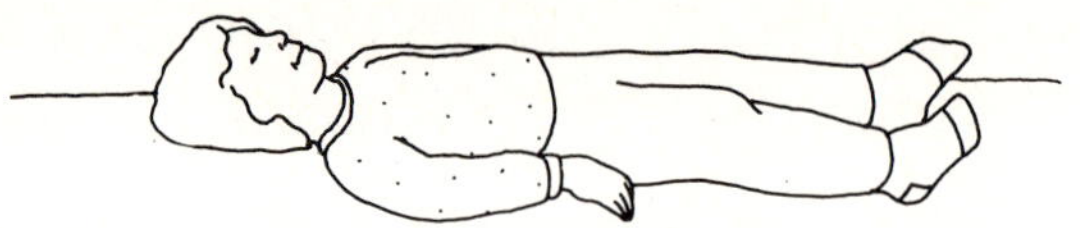

5. Stretch your arms and fingers out to the side. Hold for a moment. Then relax.

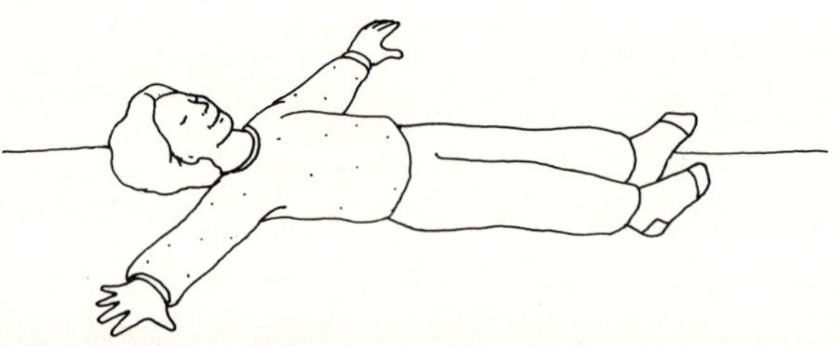

6. Lift your hips. Feel your back stretch. Now relax.

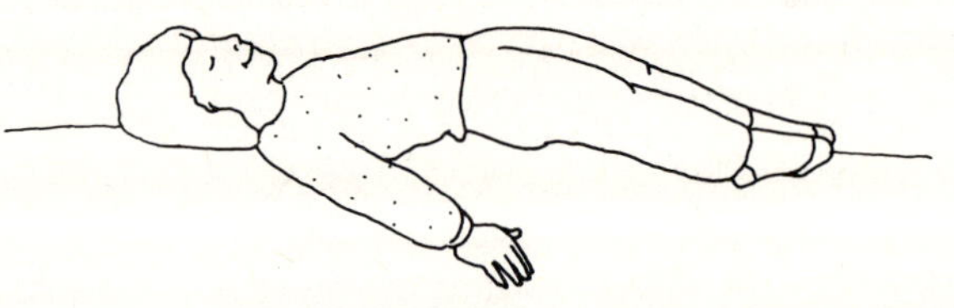

7. Keep your feet together. Stretch your legs and toes. Hold. Then relax.

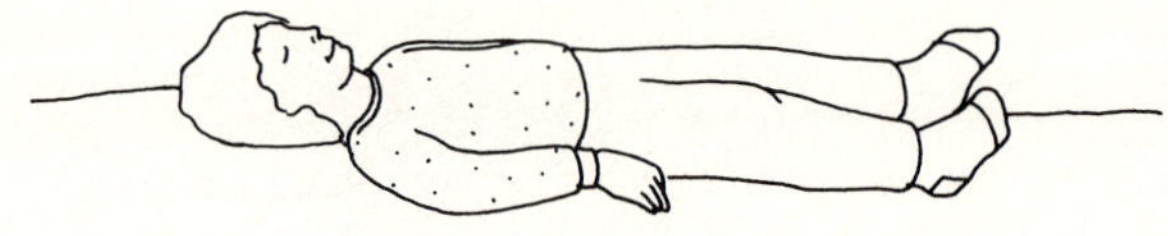

Do these exercises until you feel quite relaxed.
Then rest for a bit. Before you stand up, turn over on
your side. Rest there for a few minutes. Try to do these
exercises every day, not just when you feel tension.

Questions

1. The reading says your heart pounds when you feel
   a. relaxed.
   b. tired.
   c. tense.

2. To do the exercises in this lesson, you should
   a. lie on the floor.
   b. sit in a comfortable chair.
   c. stand up.

3. Why is it important to relax?

   ____

   ____

4. Why should you wear comfortable clothes when
   you exercise?

   ____

   ____

Think About It

Exercise is one way to relax. What are some other
ways? Make a list of ways that *you* relax.

How I Relax

1. ____
2. ____
3. ____
4. ____
5. ____

Coping: "Stopping by Woods on a Snowy Evening"

Before You Read

Read the title of the poem. Do you know this poem? The title tells you what the poem is about. Pretend you are the poet. You stop on the road next to the woods. It is snowing. Night has fallen. Write what you could see, hear, smell, or touch.

"Stopping by Woods on a Snowy Evening"

what I hear

____

____

____

what I smell

____

____

____

what I see

____

____

____

what I touch

____

____

____

Stopping by Woods on a
Snowy Evening by Robert Frost

Whose woods these are I think I know.
His house is in the village though;
He will not see me stopping here
To watch his woods fill up with snow.

My little horse must think it queer
To stop without a farmhouse near
Between the woods and frozen lake
The darkest evening of the year.

He gives his harness bells a shake
To ask if there is some mistake.
The only other sound's the sweep
Of easy wind and downy flake.

The woods are lovely, dark and deep,
But I have promises to keep,
And miles to go before I sleep.
And miles to go before I sleep.

Questions

1. Where is the man who owns the woods?
   a. in the woods
   b. in the village
   c. in another country

2. What seems queer or strange to the horse?

____

____

3. Look at the last four lines of the poem. What
   does the poet say?
   a. He likes the woods, but he must keep going.
   b. He is going to sleep in the woods.
   c. He will have to cut down trees in the woods.

4. Poems often have more than one meaning. In
   this poem, the poet talks about sleep. What else
   could the poet mean when he talks about sleep?

Think About It

How do you feel when you read this poem? Write
down a few words that tell your feelings.

__________   __________   __________

__________   __________   __________

About Robert Frost (1874–1963)

Robert Frost was forty years old when his first book of
poetry came out. For many years, his family did not
have much money. He had to work as a farmer and a
teacher. But he was always writing poems.

His poems talk about things like birth, death,
friendship, and growing up. The words are often
simple. But Frost's poems say a lot about life. He is
one of America's best-loved poets.

A Reading Tip When you see dates such as 1874–1963, you read it as "1874 to 1963."

There are two dates written after Robert Frost's name.

Robert Frost (1874–1963)

Between the two dates is a mark. It is called a dash. For the dash, you say *to*. So you read, "Robert Frost, 1874 to 1963." You can guess what the dates mean.

When was Frost born? _______________________

When did he die? _______________________

How old was Frost when he died? (Hint: you will need to subtract.) _______________________

Looking Back

Word Bank

Look over the words in your word bank. Do you remember what each one means? Choose five words from your word bank. Write sentences using these words. Have someone else read your sentences. Talk about the word meanings together. See if he or she can tell you the meaning of the word bank words.

Writing

In this unit you read about people who have different problems. You learned what they have done about their problems.

Think of a friend who has a problem. Write a letter to your friend. Tell your friend some ways that he or she could deal with the problem.

Dear _________ ,

I know you have a problem. It is that ___________
____
_______________________________________ .

Here are some things you could do about your problem. _______________________________
____
____

Your friend,

____

Talking

Look over the poems, stories, and articles you read in this unit. Pick one that you think one of your friends would like. Tell your friend about the reading. Tell your friend why you think he or she would like it.

3 Messages

People send messages to each other. How do we send
messages? We wave our hands. We call on the phone.
We write letters. We smile at someone. We shout. We
laugh. We cry. We send messages to people all day
long.

In this unit, you will read about different kinds of
messages. Some of the messages are for only one
person. Some are for everyone. As you read, think
about the special messages *you* would like to send.

Using Clues to Read New Words

Two things help you read a new word.

- the meaning of the other words and sentences around the new word
- sound clues in the new word

Here are some words you will read in Unit 3. Try using clues to read them.

1. ancestors

This word is in a poem in Unit 3.

In a secret place
our <u>ancestors</u>
the old ones with wrinkled faces
and white hair
left us these words:

The *meaning clues* to the word are in the two lines after it. Read them again and answer these questions.

Ancestors are probably
a. people
b. things

Underline the words in the poem that tell you this.

Ancestors are probably
a. younger
b. older

Therefore ancestors are the people who came
a. before us
b. after us

Circle those who are your ancestors.

parents   grandparents   children

Ancestors can also be a large group. *The ancestors of the Indians came to America over 20,000 years ago.*

Now use **sound clues** to say *ancestors*.

What is the first sound? _____
How do you say the *c*? Like an *s* or like a *k*? Try saying it both ways before you decide.

2. provide

This word is in a story about mothers whose sons are in gangs.

"They don't help me in the house, so I don't buy them anything except food," she said. "I don't know how they <u>provide</u> for themselves. I guess, like a lot of mothers, I don't want to know."

Look at the words "they provide for themselves." Fill in the missing letters.

- *They* probably means her s_n_.

- She only gives them f_ _d.

- True/False: The sons probably want other things. ___

- They must g_t other things for themselves.

- *Provide* must mean to get things.

Check this guess. Try it in the sentence: "I don't know how they <u>get things</u> for themselves."

Does it make sense? _________________________________

Now use **sound clues** to say *provide*.

What letters make the first sound? _________________

What sound does the *i* make? (Hint: The *e* is silent.)
    a. like the *i* in *hide*
    b. like the *i* in *hit*

3. surrender

You will read this word in a story about an Indian chief of the past.

> Fighting the U.S. Army all along the way, the Indians crossed Idaho and Montana. They were trapped just forty miles from Canada. After a five-day fight, they were beaten.
>
>   It was then that Chief Joseph made his speech of surrender.

What is going on?

True/False: The U.S. Army and the Indians were fighting. _________________________________

    Chief Joseph's people
    a. won
    b. lost
Underline the words that tell you this.

What do you do when you are beaten? You stop fighting, you give up, you s _ _ _ _ _ _ _ er.

    In his surrender speech, Chief Joseph probably said:
    a. "I am tired of fighting."
    b. "I will keep fighting."

You can also use **sound clues** to say this word. You can break long words like *surrender* into short sounds, or syllables. You need at least one vowel for each syllable.

The vowels in surrender—the **u, e,** and **e**—are not next to each other. This tells you each one may belong to a different syllable. Three vowels can make three syllables.

sur ren der

These three syllables are not really words. But each one is easy to say. Say them slowly, one at a time. Then say them fast. *Surrender.*

A Reading Tip A good way to read a long word is to look for small sounds, or syllables, in the word.

Here are some words divided into syllables. Try to say each word.

nap/kin   pen/cil   dan/ger   mas/ter
con/struc/tion   in/for/ma/tion

Divide these words into syllables.

magnet   dentist   wonderful
husband   internal   mention

Word Practice

Write each new word in the sentence where it fits best.

ancestors   provide   surrender

1. If you make dinner, I will __________ dessert.

2. Pierre's __________ came from France.

3. The losing army had to __________ .

Messages: "My Son" and "Mi hijo"

Before You Read

A Word to Know

ancestors The past members of a family or group. Your grandparents, great-grandparents, and so on back, are your ancestors.

This poem is written in English and in Spanish. The poet tells us what she learned from her ancestors. What is one thing you learned from your ancestors?

<table>
<tr><td>

My Son by Toni de Gerez

In a secret place
our ancestors
the old ones with wrinkled faces
and white hair
left us these words:

Look long
and wisely

Is this real?
Is this the truth?

Now
listen to my words
with care

Look at things
look long
and wisely

Is this real?
Is this true?

This is how you must work
and act

</td><td>

Mi hijo by Toni de Gerez

En un lugar secreto
nuestros antepasados
los ancianos de rostros arrugados
y cabellos blancos
nos dejaron estas palabras:

    observa largamente
      sabiamente

¿Es esto real?
¿Es esta la verdad?

Ahora
escucha mis palabras
de buen talante

Observa las cosas
observa largamente
y sabiamente

¿Es esto real?
¿Es esta la verdad?

Así es como debes de trabajar
y actuar

</td></tr>
</table>

Questions

1. Where did the ancestors leave their words?
   a. in a book
   b. in a secret place
   c. in a cave

2. What do the poet's ancestors look like?

____

3. The ancestors say we should look long and
   wisely at things. What questions should we ask
   as we look?

   ____

   ____

4. Which of these sentences tells the message of
   the poem?
   a. Look carefully at life.
   b. Do not tell lies.
   c. Everyone must work hard.

   Circle the part of the poem that tells the message.

5. What are some things in our life we should look
   at long and wisely? Make a list of them.

   ____

   ____

   ____

   ____

   ____

Think About It

People learn from their ancestors. What would you
like to teach your children and grandchildren? Write
down your ideas. Share them with someone else.

____

____

____

Asking Yourself Questions

Good readers ask questions when they read. They look for answers in the story.

Before you begin reading, predict what the story is about. Then ask questions. Here are some questions you can ask before you read.

- Who or what am I reading about?

- What do I know about this?

As you read, you'll find some answers. Then ask new questions. Here are some examples.

- What is happening?

- Why does it happen?

- What will happen next?

After you read, think about all your questions. Were they all answered? Ask these questions.

- What did I learn?

- What does it mean to me?

The next story is in three parts. As you read, think of questions for each part of the story. Some examples will be given.

Hints for Good Readers

- Before you read, think of some questions you hope the story will answer.

- As you read, look for the answers to your questions. Then ask new questions about the story.

- After you read, think about your questions. Were they all answered? What new questions do you have? Where could you find the answers?

Messages: "Mothers and Gangs, Part One"

Before You Read

Words to Know

arrest   take to jail or court

tattoo   a design made by pricking the skin and putting in colors

Words often break into syllables between double consonants. Here are some examples: sitter (sit/ter), butter (but/ter), matter (mat/ter).

Circle the double consonants in these new words.

arrest   tattoo

Now break the words between the double consonants.

arrest   tattoo

A Reading Tip Look for double consonants in new words. Double consonants help break words into syllables. They are important for spelling too.

Look at the title of this story. What do you think the story will be about?

Write down one question you think the story can answer. Here is an example: Why do young people join gangs? Now write *your* question.

Mothers and Gangs

Introduction

They love their sons. They fear for them. They are mothers whose sons are in gangs.

Most of these women raise their children alone. Most are poor. In their neighborhoods, half the children drop out of school. There are few jobs. What jobs there are pay little. Their children find more money—and excitement—in gang life.

Nights are the hardest times for these mothers. They know, when their sons go out, they may not come back. They may end up in jail or hurt or dead.

Three women told their stories to the *Chicago Tribune.* Their names have been changed. "It's too late for me," said one mother. "But maybe if we let people know about our troubles, . . . someone else's son might be saved."

Part One

Teresa

Teresa's only son was shot and killed on August 22, 1988. It was his birthday.

"I wanted someone to know what a wonderful son Tony was," she said. "He was the star of my life. It's been months since he died, but I still cry all the time. I can't even work a full week."

Teresa knew her son was no saint. "This was the third time he'd been shot. He'd been arrested for fighting. He had an earring and a tattoo. But you know what that tattoo said? It read, 'Love Ma.' "

Teresa said Tony was getting tired of the gang. "He said, 'Ma, I want to walk down the street and not be running from anybody.' " He had started night school. And he got a job. But, "he made only $3.50 an hour. His friends made fun of him. . . ."

A puppy growls. The dog, Teresa said, had been a birthday present for her son.

Questions

1. Look at the question you wrote before reading. Was your question answered? If it was, write the answer.

____

____

2. Who is this reading about?
   a. working mothers
   b. mothers of sick children
   c. mothers of children in gangs

3. Why is night the hardest time for these mothers?

   ____

   ____

4. How do you think Teresa feels about gangs?

   ____

5. Do you think Tony was a good boy? Explain.

   ____

   ____

Think About It

How do you feel about street gangs? Are there street gangs where you live? What should be done about them?

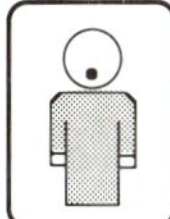

   Write a few words about your ideas. Then talk to someone else. Find out how that person feels about street gangs.

____

____

____

Messages: "Mothers and Gangs, Part Two"

Before You Read

A Word to Know

provide   to get what is needed or wanted

Read the first paragraph of Part Two. Then ask a question you think this part of the story will answer. Here's an example:

Are all four sons in a gang?

Now write your question.

<h1>Mothers and Gangs</h1>

Part Two

Lucinda

Lucinda lives on the third floor. It's a nice apartment, full of plants. Pictures of her four sons are all around. The boys are fifteen, seventeen, eighteen, and twenty. The family moved here recently. The move was Lucinda's way of getting her boys to "straighten up."

The plan has not worked. After the move, two of her sons were arrested. And every night their two brothers go back to the old neighborhood. They go there to be with the gang.

"Do my boys hurt people? They probably do. I tell them if they don't change their ways they're gonna get killed out there. They quit school. They won't work."

Lucinda's first son began to have problems six years ago. He started coming home late. He got into trouble with the police. She would yell at him. But "he'd pay me no mind," she said. "That hurt. It was like he'd found something better out there and I didn't matter."

Then two more sons joined the same gang.

"They don't help me in the house so I don't buy them anything except food," she said. "I don't know how they provide for themselves. I guess, like a lot of mothers, I don't want to know."

Questions

1. Look at the question you asked for Part Two. Was it answered? If it was, write the answer.

   ____

2. What did Lucinda do to keep her sons away from the gang?

   ____

   ____

3. Why didn't her plan work?
   a. Her sons went back to the old neighborhood.
   b. Her sons began a new gang.
   c. The old gang came to the new neighborhood.

4. What was the first sign that her oldest son had joined a gang?

   ____

5. What happened when Lucinda scolded her son?
   a. He quit the gang.
   b. He didn't listen.
   c. He moved out of the house.

Think About It

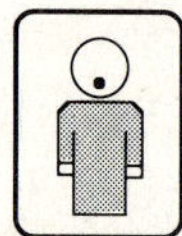

Lucinda says she doesn't want to know what her sons do in the gang. How would you feel? Would you want to know? What would you do about it?

Messages: "Mothers and Gangs, Part Three"

Before You Read

Words to Know

court   place where law cases are decided

judge   person who decides law cases

Write the new words in these sentences.

Since he broke the law, he had to go to ___________ .

He hoped the ___________ would be easy on him.

Read the first paragraph of Part Three on page 88.
Ask a question you think the story can answer.

____

____

Part Three

Julia

Julia's son is thirteen years old. Like her, Andre is small and good-looking. Julia wishes Andre didn't look like her.

This is why. Andre does something wrong. He goes to court. Then, "the judge takes one look at how little and cute he is and sends him home," Julia said. "My boy needs help. His looks are gonna get him killed."

Andre robbed an old woman. The court sent him home. A short time later, he was caught with a gun. The court sent him home again.

The next day he was shot. Julia almost "went over the edge," she said. She thought it must be a mistake. But now she wonders.

"Every time I went to visit Andre in the hospital, there were five or six grown men sitting by his bed." She knew they were drug dealers.

Andre came home. "I caught him with bags of 'reefer' [marijuana cigarettes] in his pockets."

Julia said she feels her son is lost to her. "Andre thinks he's a hero 'cause he got shot and didn't die."

Julia cries often. "I never should have moved into this building. It's so rough here, and Andre's so small. . . .

"He had to be extra bad just to get by. . . . Now I can't control him no more. I just hope that the courts take Andre away from here and get him the help he needs."

Questions

1. Look at the question you asked before reading. Was it answered? If so, write the answer.

   ____

   ____

2. Write 1, 2, 3, and 4 to show the order of these events.

   _______ a. Andre was caught with a gun.

   _______ b. Julia found Andre's "reefer."

   _______ c. Andre was shot.

   _______ d. Andre robbed an old woman.

3. Why does Julia wish Andre did not look like her?
4. What does Julia hope for Andre?
5. Do you think the courts will help Andre?

Think About It

What would you do if you were the judge? How do you think boys like Andre should be treated?

____

____

____

You have read about three mothers whose sons are in gangs. What did the mothers do to help their sons? What would *you* do? Fill in the list with your ideas.

What the mothers did	**What I would do**
1. _____________________	1. _____________________
2. _____________________	2. _____________________
3. _____________________	3. _____________________

Reading in Phrases

What is a phrase? A **phrase** is a small group of words that go together.

When we speak, we stop a little between phrases. Ask a friend to say something. Listen carefully. See if you can hear little pauses, or stops, as your friend speaks. These little pauses mark the phrases.

Reading one word at a time makes it hard to get meaning. Read this sentence to a friend. Pause five seconds after each word. (Use a watch or count to five slowly.)

I   am   reading   so   slowly   you   may
forget   what   I   am   reading.

The words in a phrase make meaning together. So it makes sense to read them together. Read this:

I am reading   so slowly   you may forget
what I am reading.

Here are some sentences from the story "Mothers and Gangs." Put a line after each phrase in these sentences. The first one is done for you.

1. They love / their sons.

2. They fear   for them.

3. They are mothers   whose sons   are in gangs.

4. Most of these women   raise their children   alone.

Commas, dashes, and periods help you make
breaks. Try reading the sentences below. Draw a line
after each phrase. The first one is done for you.

5. In their neighborhoods,/half the children drop
out of school. There are few jobs. What jobs there are
pay little. Their children find more money—and
excitement—in gang life.

Something to Think About

Look back at the poems on pages 67 and 77. Often poets like
to write just one or two phrases on a line. Why do you think
they do that?

Try reading the next story in phrases. Read the
story silently. Then read it aloud. Listen for the
pauses. Then read it again silently.

A Reading Tip Move your eyes over each whole
phrase. Stop at the end of the phrase.

Hints for Good Readers

- Read a phrase at a time. Pause between phrases.
- Look for commas, dashes, and periods to help you know
  where to pause.

Messages: "The Surrender Speech of Chief Joseph"

Before You Read

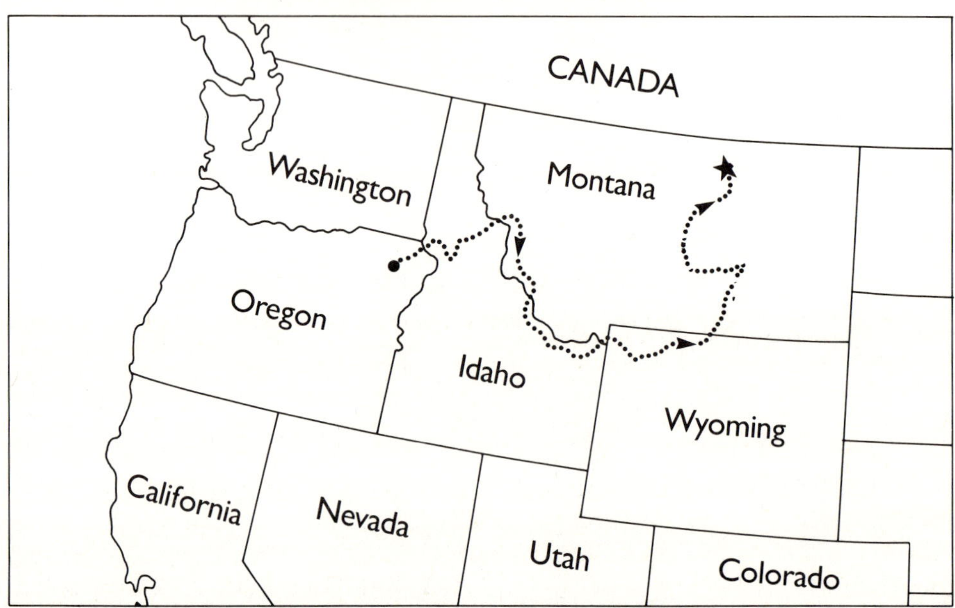

The Flight of the Nez Percé, 1877

A Word to Know

surrender   to give up

Say It Right

Nez Percé   (nez pers)

Toohulhulsote   (too HOOL HOOL zoht)

The next reading is a speech. Look at the title and the picture on page 94. Who gave this speech?

What do you think was the reason for the speech?

Try reading this speech in phrases. Draw a line after each phrase to help you.

The Surrender Speech of Chief Joseph

Joseph was chief of the Nez Percé, a Native American tribe of Oregon. In 1877 they were ordered to a reservation. They refused to go. Instead, Chief Joseph tried to lead 800 of his people to Canada. Fighting the U.S. Army all along the way, they crossed Idaho and Montana. They were trapped just forty miles from Canada. After a five-day fight, they were beaten.

It was then that Chief Joseph made his speech of surrender.

"I am tired of fighting. Our chiefs are killed. Looking Glass is dead. Toohulhulsote is dead.* The old men are all dead. It is the young men who say yes or no. He who led the young men is dead.

"It is cold and we have no blankets. The little children are freezing to death. My people, some of them, have run away to the hills and have no blankets, no food. No one knows where they are—perhaps freezing to death. I want to have time to look for my children and see how many I can find. Maybe I shall find them among the dead.

"Hear me, my chiefs. I am tired. My heart is sick and sad. From where the sun now stands, I will fight no more forever."

*Looking Glass and Toohulhulsote were Nez Percé chiefs.

Chief Joseph

Questions

1. Why did Chief Joseph want to take his tribe to Canada?

____

2. What happened to his tribe?

____

____

3. Chief Joseph says, "It is the young men who say yes or no." What does he mean?
   a. Only the young men are left to lead.
   b. The young men want to go to the reservation.
   c. All the young men have died.

4. What is Chief Joseph's message in this speech?
   a. He wants to start a war.
   b. He has named another leader of the Nez
      Percé.
   c. He will surrender to the U.S. Army.

5. How does Chief Joseph feel?

   ____

   ____

6. How do you feel when you read this speech?
   Why?

   ____

   ____

Think About It

In Unit 1, you read a speech by Martin Luther King,
Jr. He told about his dream of freedom for all people.
What do you think Chief Joseph's dream was?

____

What happened to his dream?

____

Were Chief Joseph's dream and Martin Luther
King's dream alike in any way? How?

____

____

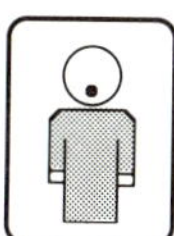

Share your ideas with someone else.

Looking Back

Word Bank

By now you should have many words in your word bank. Many of them will be from stories and articles in this book. You may also have words you heard as you talked with other people. Did you write a sentence using each word? If not, do so now.

You can group your word bank words in many ways. For example, you can make a group of words related to the law. You might include *arrest, court, judge,* and *surrender* in this group. Or you could make a group of words that describe people. You might include *hero, athlete, couple, ancestors,* and *judge* in this group.

Make a group of words that are all alike in some way. Ask someone to guess how the words are alike.

You could also make a group of hard-to-spell words. Many people have trouble spelling *straight* and *miracle.* Other hard words to spell are *shoulder* and *muscle.*

Make a group of words that are hard for you to spell. Copy each word several times. Each time you write the word, you get practice spelling it.

Writing

In this unit you have read many different messages. Some messages were for one person. Some messages were for many people.

Think of a message that you have. On the next page are some ideas.

It can be a message for just one person. That person may be someone close to you:

- a friend

- a spouse

- your child or grandchild

- your teacher

  Or someone you may never have met:

- the President of the U.S.

- the mayor of your town

- a TV or movie star

- someone who wrote a story or poem in this book

  Or it can be a message for many people:

- teenagers

- older people

- men

- women

Think about the best way to tell your message. You can write a letter, a poem, or a speech. You can write a song or a story.

Fill in the word map on the next page. The map will help you get ideas for writing. Then write your message on your own paper.

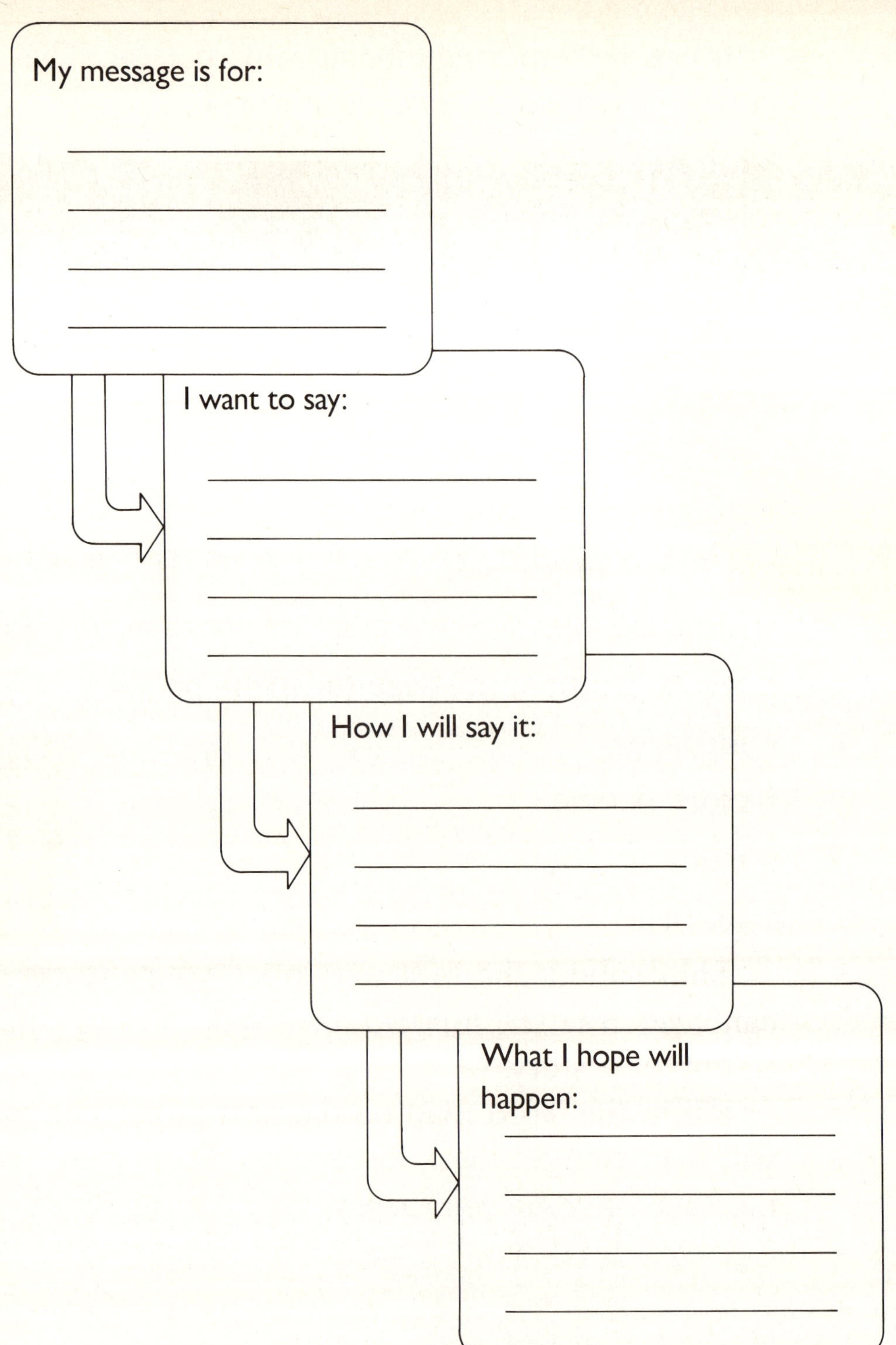

My message is for:
I want to say:
How I will say it:
What I hope will happen:

4 Cultures

There are many different cultures in the world. In every country, people have their own special traditions. They have their own stories. They have their own ways of cooking. But there is one thing everyone shares. We are all human beings.

In this unit, you will read about people from different cultures. As you read, think about your own culture. What is it like? What traditions have been important to you?

Figure It Out!

Here are some words you will see in Unit 4. Some of them may be new to you or hard to read.

guerrillas   legally   massacre

migrant workers   immigrants

These words are underlined in the story below. See if you can figure out what they mean and how to say them. Remember the five steps that will help you.

1. Read past the new word. Look at the words and sentences before and after the word.

2. Try to guess what it means.

3. Look at the first and last sounds of the word. Guess how to say the word.

4. Put Steps 2 and 3 together.

5. Check your guess. Does it make sense?

Immigrants Come to the U.S. for Many Reasons

Why do immigrants come to the United States? They come for many reasons.

Some come because their countries are poor. They want work. They want their children to have a better life.

Some come because there is war at home. Maybe they have seen the massacre of their family or friends. They are afraid they will be killed too.

Sometimes they are made to join the army. They don't like it. They are tired of fighting the <u>guerrillas</u>. They are tired of having to turn guns on their own people.

So they come and look for work in the United States. Many immigrants take jobs as <u>migrant workers.</u> Migrant workers go from place to place to find work. They work long hours in the hot sun. They make very little money.

Some immigrants are not in the United States <u>legally</u>. They live in fear of being sent back to their countries. They must be careful not to be caught.

Write each underlined word next to its meaning.

__________ 1. people who fight against the regular army

__________ 2. doing something in a way that is lawful

__________ 3. people who come from their countries to live somewhere else

__________ 4. people who travel from place to place to find work

__________ 5. the killing of a large number of people

Put these words in your word bank.

Cultures: "Rice and Rose Bowl Blues"

Before You Read

A Word to Know

interception   in football, to catch the ball when the other team tries to throw it to someone on their side

It is easier to read words like *interception* if you look at the smaller parts.

1. Break the word into syllables.

____

2. What sound does the ***tion*** make?
a. ***tun*** sound   b. ***shun*** sound

3. What sound does the *c* make?
a. an *s* sound   b. a *k* sound

You can add this word to your word bank.

Look at the title of the poem. Do you know what the Rose Bowl is? This famous football game is played in California on January first each year.

What are some things this poem could be about?

I remember the day
Mama called me in from
the football game with brothers
and neighbor boys
in our front yard

said it was time
I learned to
wash rice for dinner

glancing out the window
I watched a pass interception
setting the other team up
on our 20

*Pour some water
into the pot,*
she said pleasantly,
turning on the tap
*Rub the rice
between your hands,
pour out the clouds
fill it again*
(I secretly traced
an end run through
the grains in
between pourings)

with the rice
settled into a simmer
I started out the door
but was called back

the next day
Roland from across the street
sneeringly said he heard
I couldn't play football
anymore

I laughed loudly,
asking him
where
he'd heard
such a thing

About Diane Mei Lin Mark

Diane Mei Lin Mark is an Asian American from
Hawaii. Over the years she has worked as a reporter,
a writer, and a film producer. Her work talks about
the experiences of Asian Americans.

Questions

1. In the poem, the girl must stop playing _________.

   Her mother calls her in to _________ rice.

2. What does the poet think about while washing
   the rice?
   a. boys
   b. football
   c. cooking

3. On page 103 the poet says, "I started out the
   door but was called back." Where do you think
   she was going?

4. Why did she laugh loudly at Roland?
   a. to make him think he was wrong
   b. because she liked what he said
   c. because she didn't like football anymore

5. Look at the title again. *Blues* music is music that is sad about something. What is the poet sad about?

Think About It

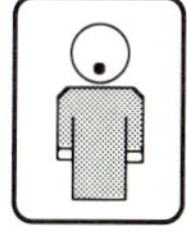

If you are a woman:
Think about when you were a little girl. Did someone ever stop you from doing something because it was "for boys"? Tell about it.

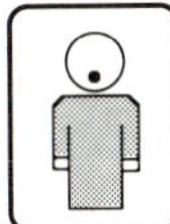

If you are a man:
Think about when you were a little boy. Did someone ever stop you from doing something because it was "for girls"? Tell about it.

Cultures: "Bad Luck!"

Before You Read

A Word to Know

Add this word to your word bank.

superstition   a belief that something can cause good luck or bad luck

What little word begins the word *superstition*?

_ _ _ _ _

What sound does **tion** make at the end of the word? Say it.

This reading is about superstitions. What is one superstition you've heard about? Write it here.

Now read to learn more about superstitions.

Bad Luck!

Break a mirror. Walk under a ladder. Notice that it's Friday the Thirteenth. What do you feel? Are you a little afraid? In all three cases, you may half-believe that you are going to have bad luck.

Such superstitions are usually very old. Often they have changed over time.

Take "knocking on wood." We do it for good luck. People long ago believed that trees were the homes of gods. So it was good luck to touch a tree. Who knows when "touching a tree" became "knocking on wood"?

Superstitions also change from place to place. The Dutch knock on wood for good luck. But it can't be painted wood. So they knock on the bottom of a table.

Look at the superstition about spilling the salt. Spilling salt brings bad luck. To stop the bad luck, throw some salt over your left shoulder. The ancient Greeks believed that. So do some people today. But . . .

Some Irish think you must throw the salt over your *right* shoulder. Or you must throw some in the fire. If you don't, you will have an argument.

And spilling the salt will cause a fight. This is an old Jewish superstition.

In Denmark, spilling wet salt is bad luck. But spilling dry salt is good luck.

In some parts of England, you must not pass the salt to another person. You set it on the table. The other person picks it up. This is probably to keep you from spilling the salt—and bringing bad luck.

Questions

1. Why did people start knocking on wood?
   a. First, people touched trees for good luck. Then they started knocking on anything made of wood.
   b. Ladders were always made of wood. People started knocking on them for good luck.
   c. The Dutch thought it would bring them good luck to touch painted wood.

2. What do the Irish believe about spilling salt?

   ____

   ____

3. Which of these things brings bad luck?

   a. spilling dry salt in Denmark
   b. throwing salt in the fire in Ireland
   c. passing the salt in England

4. Which of these sentences is true?
   a. Superstitions change over time.
   b. No one believes in superstitions anymore.
   c. Superstitions are the same everywhere.

5. Look at the picture on page 106. How many superstitions do you see in it?

Think About It

Can some things really bring you good luck or bad luck? If your answer is yes, tell about a time when something brought you good or bad luck. If your answer is no, tell why you feel this way.

____

____

____

____

Checking Your Reading

What word did this family read wrong? _______________

Mistakes often happen when people read. Good readers check what they read. They ask, "Does this make sense?"

As you read, check your reading. When something doesn't make sense, stop and think about it. Is there a word you don't understand? Do you need to read the sentence again? Do you need help? Find out what the problem is. Then think about how to solve it.

As you read the next story, check your reading. Make sure everything makes sense. The questions on the side will help you check your reading.

Hints for Good Readers

As you read, ask yourself these questions:

- Does this make sense to me?
- Is there anything I don't understand?
- How can I try to understand it?
- Am I reading carefully enough?
- Do I need to check the meaning of any words?
- Do I need more help?

Cultures: ''Ways of Dying''

Before You Read

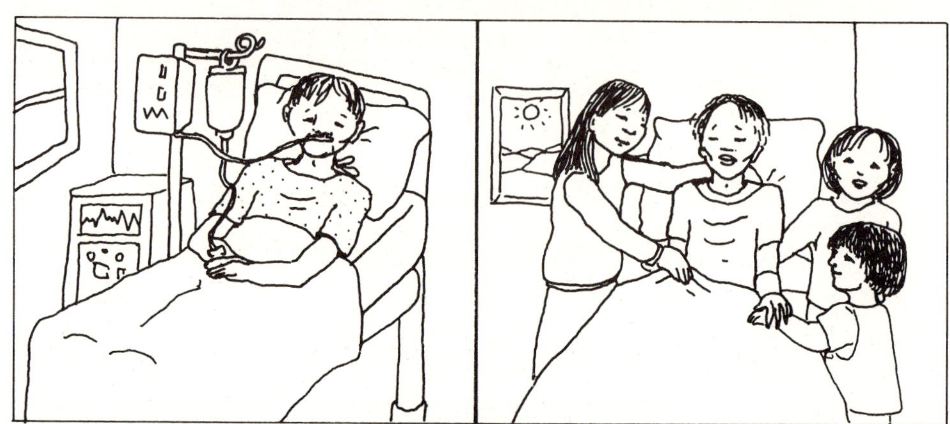

Words to Know

immigrants   people who come from a country to live in a different country

intensive care   the part of a hospital where very sick people are cared for

Look at the **-ive** at the end of *intensive*. The *i* sounds like the *i* in *lit*. It does not sound like the *i* in *five*. The *i* in **-ive** at the end of many long words sounds like the *i* in *lit*.

Put **-ive** on the ends of these words.
Read them over a few times.

1. expens_ _ _   4. defect_ _ _

2. detect_ _ _   5. reflect_ _ _

3. protect_ _ _   6. defens_ _ _

Look over the reading. Read the title. Look at the pictures. What do you think it will be about? Write your prediction here.

____

Now read to see if your guess was right.

Ways of Dying

Do you know what *adapt* means?

Many people come to the United States from other countries. They find things different here. Young people soon adapt. They quickly learn American ways, American ideas.

Older people often find it harder. They have lived a long time with the old ways. The new ways can frighten them.

Dying the American way is one thing that frightens many of them. Here, we hide the dying. People die in hospitals. Often they are in intensive care. Family and friends find it hard to visit. Older immigrants fear these "dying rooms."

Do you understand why they fear American hospitals?

In many other countries, people die at home. The family is present. Friends visit. A sixty-year-old Laotian man tells this story:

"My grandfather died in the house. All the family was inside, the children too. My parents told us that we were going to say good-bye to Grandpa because we were never going to see him again. 'He is going to eternity,' my mother said. Some people wept. One of my uncles said, 'I am never going to see you again.' And then he cried. The neighbors visited. The grandchildren said to the old man, 'Many thanks for taking care of us, for not leaving us.'"

How is this different from dying in America?

Many older immigrants miss the close ties of the old ways. In the United States, they do not know their neighbors. Their aunts and uncles are far away. They are lonely. They fear a lonely death. At least, they say, they want to be buried with people from their own country. They want to die with dignity.

Questions

1. What does this reading explain about people from other countries?
   a. why they get sick when they come to the United States
   b. why they are afraid of dying in the United States
   c. why they will never go to hospitals

2. Why is it easier for young people to learn American ways?

   ____

   ____

   ____

3. Why do older immigrants fear dying in the United States?

   ____

   ____

   ____

4. How is dying different in other countries?
   a. People live longer.
   b. No one visits people who are dying.
   c. People often die at home.

Think About It

What are some other things people have to get used
to when they come to the United States? Add your
ideas to the map.

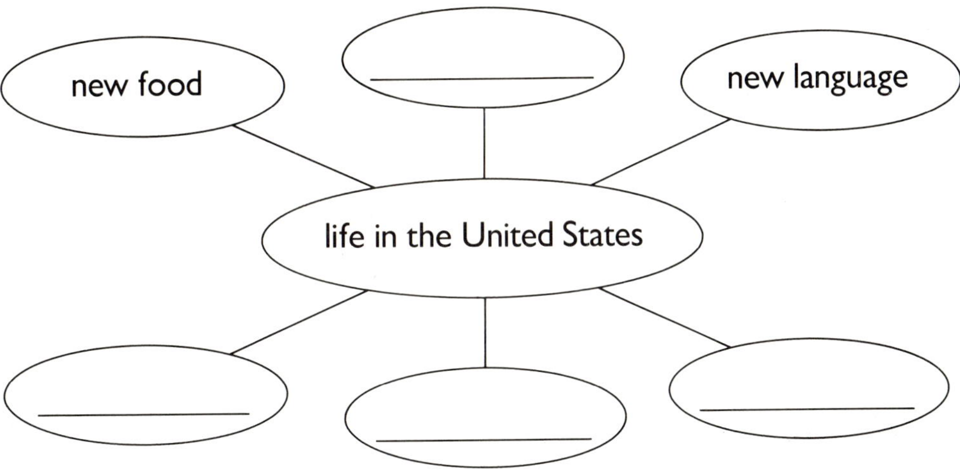

Cultures: "Indiantown, Part One"

Before You Read

Words to Know

guerrillas (guh RIHL uhs) a band of soldiers who fight against the regular army

massacre the killing of a large number of people

Say It Right

Guatemala (gwah teh MAH lah)

Kanjobal (kahn hoh BAHL)

This story has three parts. When you finish it, you will have read quite a lot! Look over Part One. Read the titles and the introduction on page 115. Look at the map on page 116. What do you think this story will be about?

____

____

____

Write down one question you have about Part One of the story. Then read to see if your question is answered.

____

____

____

Indiantown

Part One: "There is a place called Florida."

In Guatemala, Francisco and Isabela Ramírez were shepherds. They are Kanjobal, descendants of the ancient Mayans. They have long known poverty. Now war has come to their country too.

FRANCISCO: In 1981, soldiers came into La Cholaj, a neighboring village. They told the people, "You are Indians and you are guerrillas." They pushed forty people—men, women, and two children—into a house that they used as a prison. One old lady came to the soldiers and begged, "Please, let go of my son—he is innocent." The soldiers said, "You too. Go inside." Then they poured gasoline on the house and set it on fire. Hours later, only ashes remained of the people.

After the massacre in La Cholaj, we became very afraid. Our whole family decided to walk to Mexico. . . . Our group was 34 people, including some relatives and friends. . . .

As we prepared to leave Guatemala, we saw army helicopters patrolling the mountains along the border. I knelt down and prayed to the Lord, "Please, dear God, my wife and children and I have never done any bad things. Send us Your blessings. Help us to find a place to go to work. We need to live and find a better situation to survive as a family."

We got up off our knees and continued walking toward the Mexican countryside. At that time, we didn't know anything about the United States or Indiantown.

The Ramírez family entered Mexico in 1981. For one year they worked on a coffee plantation. Then they went north to Baja California, a state in Mexico. There, for three years, they worked on a large farm. But there were problems. They worked long hours. There was no water. There was no school for the children. In 1985 someone said, "There is a place called Florida where you can find jobs."

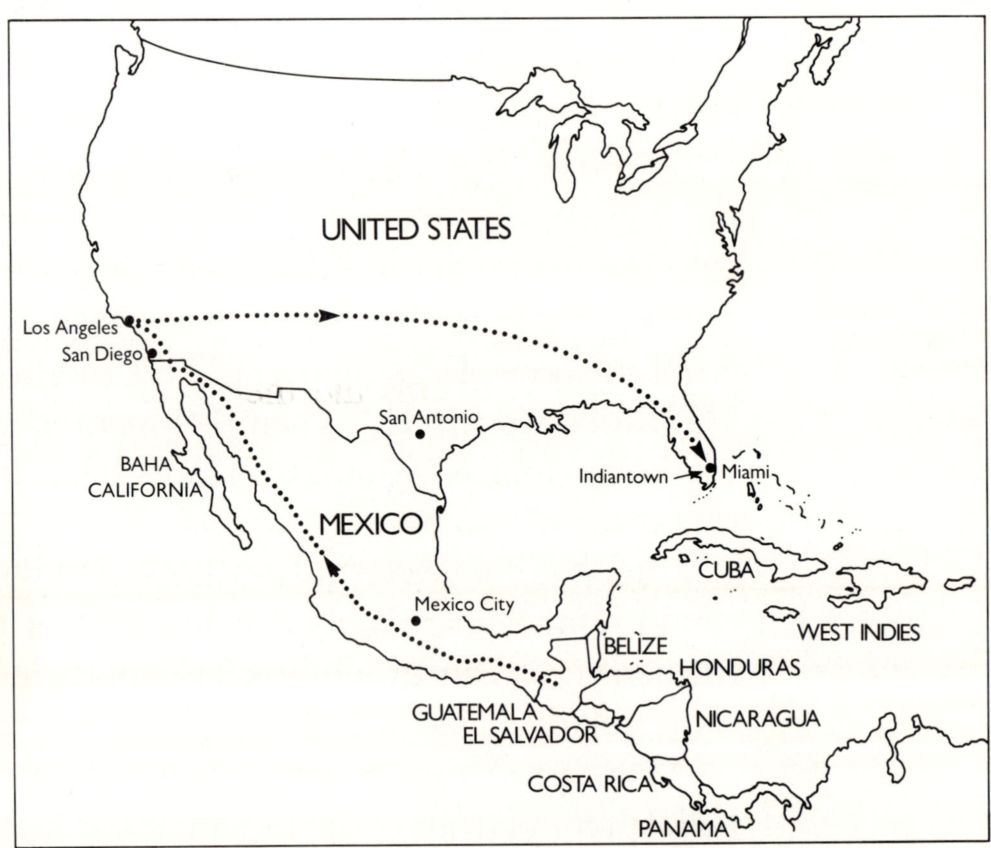

Route the Ramírez family took from Guatemala to Baja California to Los Angeles to Indiantown.

Questions

1. Look at the question you asked about Part One. Was it answered? If so, write the answer here.

   ____

   ____

2. What reason did the soldiers give for killing people?
   a. The soldiers said the people were innocent.
   b. The soldiers said the people were Indians and guerrillas.
   c. The soldiers said the people were trying to leave Guatemala.

3. What did the Ramírez family decide to do?

   ____

4. What problems did they have in Baja California?

   ____

   ____

5. What do you think will happen in Part Two?

   ____

   ____

Think About It

People leave their countries for many reasons. The Ramírez family left because they were in danger. They wanted to be safe. What are some other reasons people leave? Write your ideas on the map.

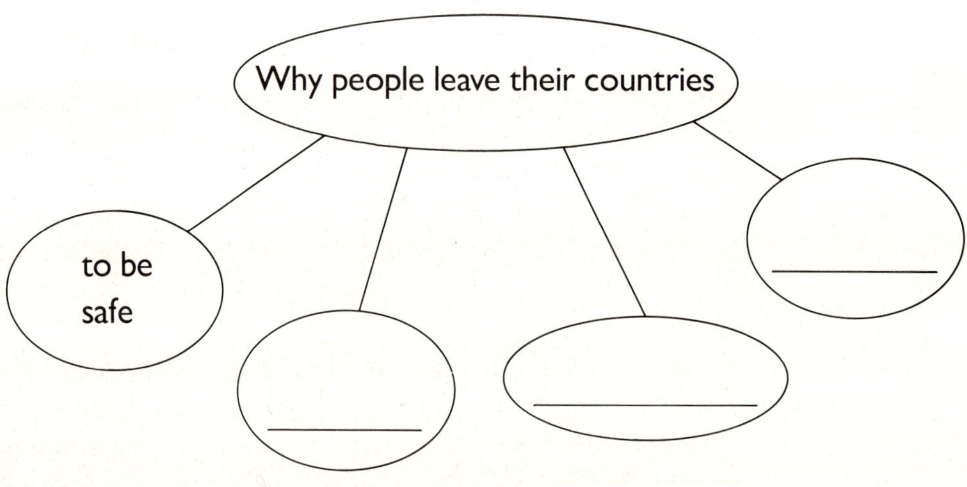

Cultures: "Indiantown, Part Two"

Before You Read

Los Angeles

Read the first paragraph of Part Two. What problems does the family have?

What are some things that could happen to them?

Now read to find out what happens to the family.

Part Two: "We had never seen a big city."

Francisco and Isabela decided to go to the United States. But they had no papers. They were afraid of being sent back to Guatemala. Another Kanjobal told them, "The army is still killing people" in Guatemala. So they and their three children snuck across the border. The Border Patrol did not see them. But they ran out of food and water.

FRANCISCO: We were very tired and had no idea where we were.

We didn't have any bread or water. We looked horrible and felt like we were dying, especially the children. It was an act of God that we met an American man. He talked to us in English. We couldn't understand his language, but he looked like a good man. It sounded like he was saying, "Where do you come from? Who are you?" We couldn't answer, but we tried talking in our language.

He said, "Ahh. I understand. You are very poor people. I can help you." He gave us some water and green lime fruit from a bag that he carried. He gave our small boy, Domingo, some candies.

After the man left, we prayed and thanked God. This man saved our lives. Then we continued walking. A few hours later, we approached the city of San Isidro. A car pulled up to us, driven by a Mexican. We didn't have any American money, but the man offered to drive us near the town. Once there, we met another Mexican, who drove us two hundred miles or more to Los Angeles. We had never seen a big city before. It was eleven o'clock at night when we arrived. All the lights were on, like a million stars. I said, "Thank God we are in Los Angeles."

Questions

1. Why didn't the Ramírez family want to go back to Guatemala?
   a. They didn't have enough money.
   b. They had no food or water.
   c. They were afraid they would be killed.

2. Francisco says the American man saved their lives. How did he do that?

   ____

   ____

3. Write 1, 2, 3, and 4 to show the order of these events.

   ______ a. The family crossed the border.

   ______ b. The family saw the lights of Los Angeles.

   ______ c. They met an American man.

   ______ d. A Mexican man drove them to San Isidro.

4. How do you think the family felt when they saw Los Angeles for the first time?

   ____

   ____

Think About It

People helped the Ramírez family. Why do you think
they helped them?

____

____

    Do you think most people would help someone
they didn't know? Explain.

____

____

Cultures: "Indiantown, Part Three"

Before You Read

Francisco and Isabela Ramírez

Words to Know

migrant workers people who must travel to different places to find work

legally doing something in a way that obeys the law

Here is Part Three of the story. Read the first paragraph. How do you picture Indiantown? What would you see? What would you hear and smell? What would people in Indiantown look like?

Read Part Three and picture what life in Indiantown is like.

Part Three: At Blue Camp

The Ramírez family made its way across the country to Indiantown, Florida, about 100 miles north of Miami. The town has 3,000 people. Every winter, 3,000 migrant workers come to pick fruit and vegetables. They are Mexicans, Haitians, Jamaicans, Puerto Ricans. Some are here legally. Many are not. About 1,000 Kanjobal live in Indiantown. Most live at Blue Camp, "a two-story, concrete ghetto."

ISABELA: Whatever we earn is usually spent on rent, food, and clothing. Sometimes we spend $100 on the family's food. Because Indiantown is a migrant farm-worker area, prices are very high. . . . And our household has grown to seven adults, two small boys, and Micaela's baby. . . .

FRANCISCO: Where do we all sleep with only one bedroom and this small kitchen-living room? We have two cots in the living room, one cot in the bedroom for Isabela and me, and the children sleep on mattresses on the floor. . . . For entertainment we have a guitar to sing Christian songs together, and a cassette player. . . . José bought an old sewing machine that the women are learning on.

ISABELA: And we have a small washing machine— we don't have to go to the river. (Laughs) . . .

FRANCISCO: The importance of living here is that we've found a relatively peaceful place, where the army isn't looking for us. In Indiantown we haven't any problems with the police. We are Christians. We go to church on Saturday, Sunday. We ask the strength of God to be better people every day. We only hope to work so that we can buy some food and clothes.

ISABELA: It's better here because we are alive. Nobody is trying to kill us.

Questions

1. Why do migrant workers come to Indiantown?

____

2. How does the Ramírez family spend their money?
   a. on entertainment
   b. on rent, food, and clothing
   c. on travel

3. Why do you think prices are high in Indiantown? Why would store owners charge more for rent, food, and clothing in a migrant farmworker area?

4. Isabela says "we don't have to go to the river." What does she mean?
   a. They don't live by a river anymore.
   b. They don't like to swim.
   c. They don't have to wash their clothes in the river.

5. What does the family like about living in Indiantown?

____

____

Think About It

You have read about the Ramírez family. They came into the United States without a visa. They were not here legally. If they were caught, they would have been sent back to Guatemala. They might have been killed.

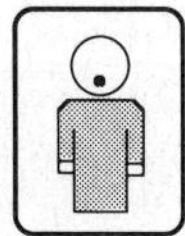

Do you think the United States should let people stay when they come without a visa? Why or why not? Write a few sentences about your ideas. Then share your thoughts with someone else.

Looking Back

Word Bank

Look back at the new words on page 123. See if you still remember what each word means. Then look over all the words you have in your word bank. Which ones do you know? Put them in one group. Which ones do you need to practice? Put them in another group.

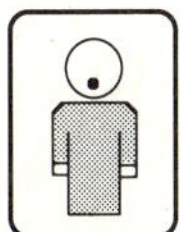

If you are in a class, compare your word bank with another student's word bank. Do you both have the same words? Are your word banks grouped in the same ways? Talk about your word bank words with the other student. You may learn some new words.

Writing

In this unit you have read about many different cultures. You have read about some of the different traditions in those cultures.

Families have traditions too. A family may have a special way of celebrating birthdays or weddings. Maybe there are some family stories that are told over and over.

Think about a tradition your family has. Write a few words about this tradition on the word map on the following page.

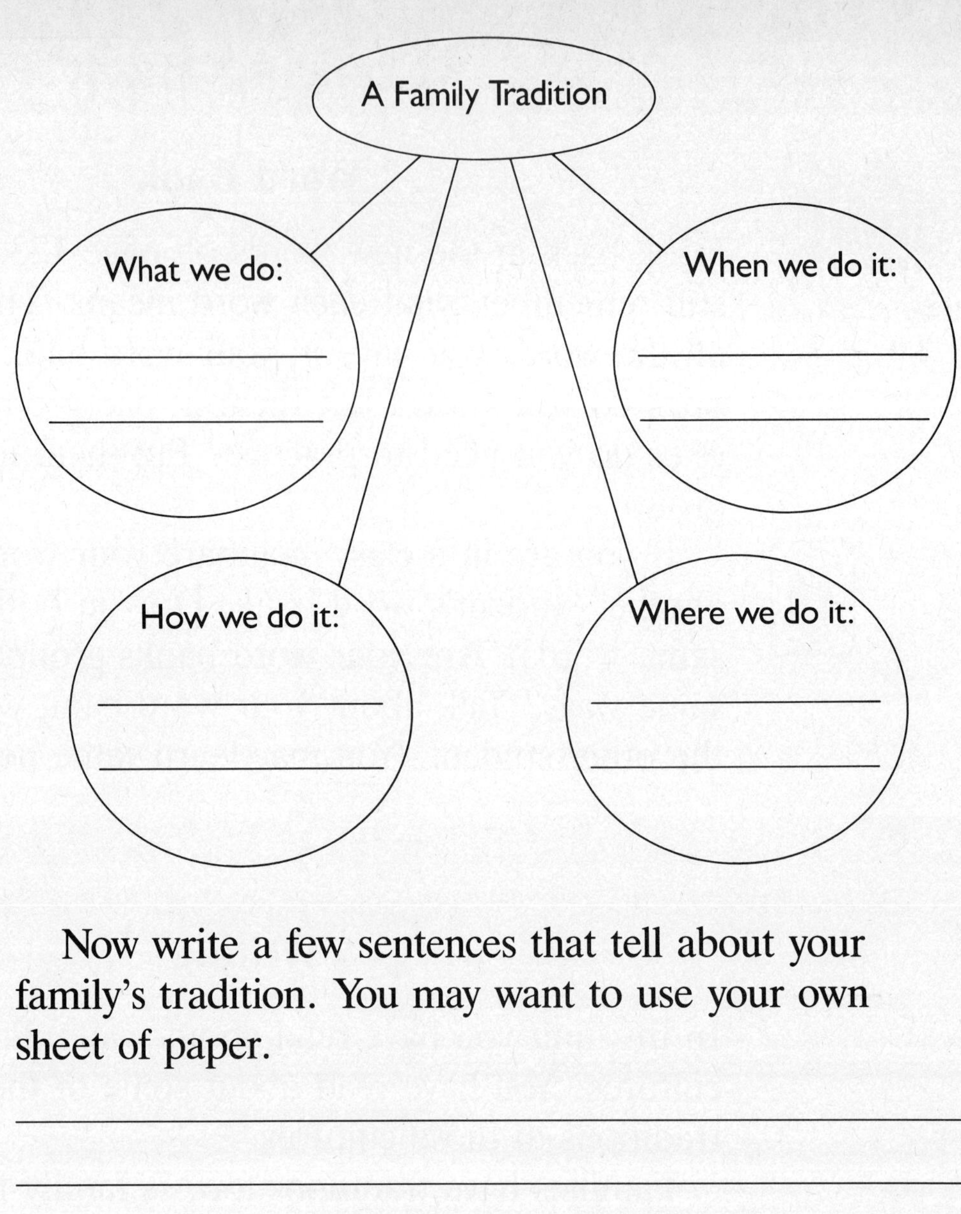

Now write a few sentences that tell about your family's tradition. You may want to use your own sheet of paper.

Final Hints for Good Readers

In this book, you have learned to use what you already know when you read. You have learned to make predictions and to picture what you read. You have learned to look for the main idea and important details.

You have learned to check your reading and to ask questions as you read. You have learned to read in phrases. In other words, you have learned the steps for becoming a good reader.

Here is a checklist of the steps you learned in this book. Try to practice at least one of them every time you read!

Before You Read

- Look ahead at the reading. Read the titles. Look at the pictures. What is the reading about?
- Think about what you already know about the topic.
- Decide why you are reading. Think of a question the reading could answer.

As You Read

- Try to picture what is happening.
- Think about what could happen next.
- Ask yourself questions about the reading. Does everything make sense?
- Try reading in phrases.

After You Read

- Tell the main idea of the reading. Do you remember the most important details?

End-of-Book Test:
"The Flying Africans"

Before You Read

A Word to Know

slavery   when human beings are owned by other
people and can be bought and sold

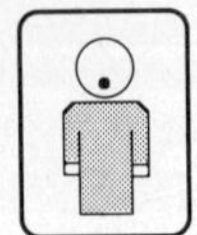

This folktale is about slavery. You probably already
know some things about slavery. Tell someone what
you know about slavery.

The Flying Africans

Used to be, Africans could fly. Not all, only some. But they lost their wings. Lost them when the people got taken for slavery, some say.

In the Sea Islands was a cruel Master. He was hard, hard on slaves. Worked them near to death.

One day he put some new-bought Africans in the fields. All day they worked. The sun burned down. There was no pause for drink or rest.

One young woman had a baby, just born. It was tied on her back. Pretty soon, she fell. Brought down by work, you know.

The Driver whipped her. A tall old man came and helped her up. They spoke some words.

After a while, she fell again. The Driver cut her with the whip. She turned to the old man.

"Is it time, Father?" she asked.

"Yes, Daughter," he said. Then he spoke some magic words. And he stretched out his arms.

Up she flew, holding her baby. Over the fields and fences. Away.

The Driver saw, but he could not believe. He whipped the others. "Back to work!" he cried.

Then a man fell, sick with work. The Driver whipped him. But he turned to the old man. The old man, as before, stretched out his arms. He said the magic words. Up went the man, flying away.

"It's you, Old Devil," cried the Driver. And he ran to whip the old man. But the old man just laughed. He said the words again.

And do you know? Every African stepped up in the air. Then they were climbing. Then swimming, then riding. They were flying like black birds. The old man was with them.

In a moment, they were gone. Where they went, no one knows for sure. Probably to Freedom.

Questions

1. When does the story say the Africans lost their wings?
   a. when they grew older
   b. when they became slaves
   c. when they worked

2. Why did the woman with the baby fall?
   a. The Driver whipped her.
   b. The work was too hard.
   c. She tried to fly too soon.

3. How did the old man help people fly?

   ____

   ____

4. The Driver tried to whip the old man. But the old man just laughed. Why do you think he laughed?

   ____

   ____

5. Why did all the Africans want to fly away?

   ____

   ____

6. Some people say the old man was really God. If the old man was God, could it mean something else to say the people flew away? Explain.

Just for Fun

This story has no questions with it. It is for you to enjoy and think about. The story is longer than the other readings in this book. You are ready for a longer story because you have learned a lot about reading in this book.

People Like Us

Al Stone and Sara Malkovich were friends. They always had been. Their families had been friends. Al's father had owned a hardware store. Sara's father had owned the grocery store next to it. Business had been great in their day.

Later, Al took over his father's store. Sara and her husband, Joe, ran the grocery. They were very proud of their businesses. They wanted to do well like their fathers.

Maybe fifteen years ago, they had. Business had been very good for Al and for Joe and Sara. But over the years, it had slowed down. Now, it was not good at all. A few years ago Joe died. Now Al and Sara were worried. They talked about the changes often.

Al said no one was to blame. "Times are bad all over," he would say. "That's why our business is bad."

But Sara didn't see it that way. "It's those foreigners in the neighborhood," she would say. "They're taking over. They've made our customers move."

Many people felt like Sara. Some did more than just talk. They broke windows on the stores of the new neighbors. They sprayed paint on the doors. The neighborhood was full of fear and anger.

One day Al came to Sara's store. He didn't come to buy anything. They just talked. They talked about old times.

"Remember? This store was the neighborhood center," Al said.

"I sure do," Sara answered. "Everybody came here for something. Kids bought candy after school. They stuffed their mouths full. They ate it all so their parents wouldn't know about it."

"Not my kids," Al said.

"Your kids were the worst," Sara told him. They laughed.

As they talked, Al noticed something. It was by the door. There was a table. It had some papers on it. Above it, there was a little sign.

"What's that?" Al asked.

"That's my petition," Sara answered. "Will you sign it?"

"A petition for what?" Al asked.

"To keep them from buying any more shops around here," Sara said. Suddenly Sara was angry.

Al was puzzled. "Them?" he asked. "Who do you mean?"

Sara was getting angrier. "You know who I mean! I've told you before. They are taking over our neighborhood. They wear strange clothes. They don't speak English. And they cook smelly food."

"Smelly food?" Al asked, with a smile. That reminded him of something.

"Yes!" Sara said. "It's hard enough running the store now that Joe is gone. I can't stand to see everything changing."

Sara was very angry. She was walking back and forth. But Al was still thinking about the "smelly food." "That's interesting," he said. He rubbed his chin. He was thinking.

"What's interesting?" Sara asked. She stopped walking for a minute.

"That's what they used to say about my uncle's restaurant."

"That was different," Sara said.

Al thought back to the stories he had heard. They were stories of hard times. It was not easy for immigrants. People did not want them around. So they stuck together. They spoke the old language. They tried to keep their culture alive.

"No, Sara. It wasn't so different," Al answered.

"Yes, it was," said Sara. "Our people had their special restaurants and stores. But they tried to become Americans too. Lots of them even changed their names. Your grandfather wasn't Stone. But when he got here, that's what he became. You don't see that with these people. They keep their strange names. They want everything to change for them. Well, this neighborhood isn't going to change for them!"

Al was surprised at Sara. He couldn't believe she was so angry. But he couldn't let her go. What she was saying reminded him too much of the old stories. He didn't want those stories happening again.

"Tell me something, Sara," Al said. "You say you don't want them around. So who do you want?"

"People like us," Sara said.

"People who work hard?" Al asked.

"Yes."

"People who are trying to make something of themselves?" Al continued.

"Yes," Sara said.

Al smiled again. "Well, isn't that what they are? Come on, Sara. People made it hard for our folks. Don't you be the one making it hard for these people."

"But this is our neighborhood!" Sara complained.

"I agree," Al said. "But it's their neighborhood too now. They are people like us. More like us than you think."

136

Sara was quiet. Al looked at her. He tried to look past the anger in her face. He tried to find his friend's face there.

But he found only a stranger's face. Sara stared back at him coldly. "Get out of my store," she said. "I never thought I'd hear you talk like this."

Al left Sara's store sadly. The neighborhood had changed, all right, he thought. The store he loved to go to, the friend he had in Sara. It was all changed, all gone.

Answers

Unit 1   People

■ A Hero   page 7

1. In 1985, Mexico City was hit by strong <u>earthquakes.</u> Many people were killed when they were trapped under <u>buildings</u>. Marcos Efrén Zariñana helped rescue many <u>people</u> after the earthquakes. Because he is <u>small</u>, he could get under the fallen buildings. He <u>rescued</u> twenty-seven people.

2. a. because he was small and thin. The flea is a very small bug.

b. Marcos helped rescue people.

c. He was small enough to get into tight spaces.

3. Sample headline: Hero Rescues 27 People After Earthquakes in Mexico

■ Jaime Escalante, Super Teacher   page 13

1. b, c, and **e** are true. Choice *a* is not true because Escalante was born in Bolivia. Choice *d* is not true because his students showed they had not cheated on the math test.

2. a. He wanted to get the students to pay attention. He knew they would learn more that way.

■ Because   page 16

1. a. She is talking to a son and a daughter in the poem.

2. Many answers are possible.

■ I Have a Dream   page 25

1. c. He wanted every person everywhere to be free.

2. b. He says he dreams his children will not be judged by their color. He wants them to be judged by "the content of thcir character." He does *not* say they shouldn't be judged at all.

3. Answers will vary. Be sure to give a reason for your answer.

■ Martin Luther King and Lincoln Monument: Washington   page 28

1. She likes him a lot. He makes her sing.

2. Many answers are possible.

3. Possible answer: She thinks of ways to work for civil rights.

4. b. He goes to see the Lincoln Memorial in Washington, D.C. The title of the poem helps you know that.

5. Possible answer: The statue will always remind us of what Lincoln believed in.

6. a. AL; Abraham Lincoln died in 1865, more than 100 years ago. Martin Luther King died in the 1960s.
b. Both; both men fought for freedom.
c. Both; both Lincoln and King were shot by gunmen.
d. AL; Abraham Lincoln was President but Martin Luther King was not.

■ Grandma Moses   page 32

1. Answers will vary. Talk about what you see with someone.

2. because he liked them

3. c. She had to find enough paintings for Mr. Caldor. She did want to sell her paintings to him, so *a* and *b* are wrong.

4. Grandma Moses liked to <u>paint.</u> She painted pictures of <u>country</u> life. One day, Louis J. Caldor saw her <u>paintings</u> in a store. He wanted to <u>buy</u> ten of them. Grandma Moses did not have <u>ten</u> paintings. She <u>cut</u> a big painting in half. Then she had ten paintings to <u>sell</u> to Mr. Caldor.

Unit 2   Coping

■ Learning New Words   page 36

1. A baton is a <u>stick</u> used in a race.

2. b. A discount means to pay less.

3. b. *Tension* probably means feeling unhappy and tight.

■ How to Save Money   page 40

1. c. If you buy some extra soap now at a good price, you will save money later. Choice *a* is wrong because even if you spend no money on soap now, you will have to buy it later. Choice *b* is wrong because if you buy only one bar now, you will need soap again soon. Next time you buy it you will probably pay more.

2. c. Frozen dinners cost more than home-made ones, so you don't save money.

3. In the fall, people don't use air conditioners. Stores lower their prices so people will still buy them.

4. Answers will vary. Some things you can do for free are going to summer fairs and having picnics.

5. Answers will vary. Three ways to save money on food are save coupons, buy fruits and vegetables when prices are lower, and make your lunch and take it to work.

■ **Jim Abbott, Rookie on the Rise   page 45**

Margin Notes page 45
young and <u>strong</u>
<u>good athlete</u>
<u>gold medal</u>
born with no <u>right hand</u>
how Jim <u>fields</u>
Jim's <u>dreams</u>
Questions   page 46
Main Idea: Jim Abbott has one hand. He is a pitcher for the California Angels.
Detail: Jim's age is <u>21</u>.
Detail: Jim won an Olympic <u>gold medal</u>.
Detail: Jim's parents <u>treated</u> him like any other <u>boy</u>.
Detail: Jim changes his glove to his <u>left hand</u> to catch.

■ **Dream Variation   page 49**

1. Both the poet and the night are black.

2. Answers will vary.

3. Many answers are possible.

4. Answers will vary. It sounds like the poet is not free to enjoy life the way he wants.

■ **How Much Is Smoking Hurting You?   page 52**

1. c. You can tell because the name of the quiz is "How Much Is Smoking Hurting You?"

2. 10 points. You get 10 points for smoking between 1 and 9 cigarettes a day.

3. No. Five cigarettes a day is ten points. The quiz says a score of ten points means your health is in danger.

4. b. The person says, "No matter how much you smoke, you should stop."

5. a. T. **b.** F—The quiz says your health will get better when you quit smoking. **c.** F—"High tar" cigarettes score more points, so they must be bad for your health. **d.** T—Smoking a pipe is 2 points. Smoking any cigarettes is 10 points or more.

■ **Sleep, Baby, Sleep   page 57**

1. a. They are trying to sleep and are very tired.

2. b. The husband says, "He's too old to still be having night feedings."

3. He thinks the baby wants to know his parents are there.

4. because the baby won't sleep

5. No. He thinks about how the baby can't help crying. He thinks about how he loves his family.

■ **Miracle in Rome   page 61**

1. b. The story says that when she was four, she got sick. Afterwards, she could not move her left leg.

2. a. 1; **b.** 3; **c.** 4; **d.** 2. Check the story if you have the order wrong.

3. c. The story says at the end that Wilma had won her third gold medal. This means that she won the race.

4. because years before, doctors had said she might never walk again

■ Relax with Exercise   page 65

1. c. Tension makes your heart beat faster. When you are relaxed or tired, it slows down.

2. a. The reading says you should lie down.

3. because too much tension can harm the body

4. so you can move more easily

■ Stopping by Woods on a Snowy Evening   page 67

1. b. The poem says, "His house is in the village though."

2. They have stopped where there are no houses. The poem says, "My little horse must think it queer/To stop without a farmhouse near."

3. a. The poet says he has "miles to go" before he sleeps, so he must keep going.

4. Answers will vary. The poet could also be talking about death.

■ Using Clues to Read New Words   page 72

1. Ancestors are probably *a.* people. In the poem, the words "the old ones with wrinkled faces/and white hair" tell you this. Ancestors are probably *b.* older. Therefore ancestors are the people who came *a.* before us. You should circle parents and grandparents. The first sound is *a.* The *c* in *ancestors* sounds like an *s.*

2. *They* probably means her <u>sons</u>. She only gives them <u>food</u>. <u>True</u>: The sons probably want other things. They must <u>get</u> other things for themselves. *Pr* makes the first sound. The *i* in *provide* makes a sound *a.* like the *i* in *hide.*

3. <u>True</u>: The U.S. Army and the Indians were fighting. Chief Joseph's people *b.* lost. The words are *trapped, beaten,* and *surrender.* You stop fighting, you give up, you <u>surrender</u>. Chief Joseph probably said *a.* "I am tired of fighting." Here is how to divide these words:
   mag/net   den/tist   won/der/ful
   hus/band   in/ter/nal   men/tion

Word Practice

1. provide **2.** ancestors **3.** surrender

■ My Son/Mi hijo   page 77

1. b. The poem says the ancestors "left us these words" in a "secret place."

2. They have wrinkled faces and white hair. They are old.

3. Is this real? Is this true?

4. a. The poem does not talk about telling lies, so *b* is wrong. The poem does not talk about work, so *c* is wrong. The poem talks about looking "long and wisely" at life.

5. Many answers are possible.

■ **Mothers and Gangs, Part One   page 82**

1. Answers will vary. It's all right if your question was not answered. Asking a question helps you read the story more carefully.

2. c. The three women in the story each have children in gangs.

3. because night is when their sons go out. The mothers are afraid their sons will be hurt or killed or end up in jail.

4. She probably hates the gangs, since her son was killed while in a gang.

5. Answers will vary. Be sure to give a reason for your answer.

■ **Mothers and Gangs, Part Two   page 86**

1. Answers will vary.

2. Lucinda moved to a new neighborhood.

3. a. The story says that every night her sons went back to the old neighborhood.

4. He started coming home late and got in trouble with the police.

5. b. Choice *a* is wrong because her son stayed in the gang. Choice *c* is wrong because her sons still live at home.

■ **Mothers and Gangs, Part Three   page 89**

1. Answers will vary.

2. a. 2; **b.** 4; **c.** 3; **d.** 1. Check the story if you have the events in the wrong order.

3. Julia thinks the judge is too easy on Andre because he is little and cute. She wants the courts to take him so he can get help.

4. Julia hopes the courts will take Andre away and get him help.

5. Answers will vary.

■ **Reading in Phrases   page 90**

1. They love/ their sons.

2. They fear/ for them.

3. They are mothers/ whose sons/ are in gangs.

4. Most of these women/ raise their children/ alone.

5. There are different ways to divide readings into phrases. This is one way you could do it. In their neighborhoods,/ half the children/ drop out/ of school./ There are/ few jobs./ What jobs there are/ pay little./ Their children find/ more money/— and excitement—/ in gang life./

■ **The Surrender Speech of Chief Joseph   page 94**

1. because he didn't want the tribe to be moved to a reservation

2. His tribe was trapped by the U.S. Army. They were beaten. Many died. Chief Joseph had to surrender.

3. a. He says that all the old men are dead. So only the young men are left to lead.

4. c. He says he will never fight again.

5. tired, sick, and sad

6. Answers will vary.

Unit 4   Cultures

■ **Figure It Out!   page 101**

1. guerrillas

2. legally

3. immigrants

4. migrant workers

5. massacre

■ **Rice and Rose Bowl Blues   page 102**

A Word to Know   page 102

1. in ter cep tion

2. b. It makes the *shun* sound.

3. a. It makes the *s* sound.

Questions   page 104

1. In the poem, the girl must stop playing <u>football</u>. Her mother calls her in to <u>wash</u> rice.

2. b. She thinks about "an end run through the grains" while washing the rice.

3. She was probably going back out to play football.

4. a. She would not like to hear that she couldn't play anymore, so *b* is wrong. You know she really liked to play football, so *c* is also wrong.

5. She is sad because she can't play football.

■ **Bad Luck!   page 108**

1. a. The reading says people thought gods lived in the trees. That is why they liked to touch trees. Next they started knocking on wood.

2. The Irish believe that if you spill salt, you should throw more salt over your right shoulder to stop bad luck. You should throw salt in the fire or you will have an argument.

3. c. Spilling dry salt in Denmark brings good luck, so *a* is wrong.

Throwing salt in the fire in Ireland prevents bad luck, so *b* is wrong.

4. a. The reading tells how superstitions are different in different places, so *c* is wrong. It also says that people still believe in them, so *b* is wrong.

5. spilled salt, a broken mirror, and a black cat crossing the road

■ Ways of Dying   page 112

1. b. The reading does not say they always get sick, so *a* is wrong. It does not say they never go to hospitals, so *c* is also wrong.

2. Young people have not lived with the old ways for very long. They are not as frightened by new American ways.

3. Answers will vary. People are afraid of hospitals. They won't be able to say good-bye to friends and family. Dying in a hospital can be lonely.

4. c. The reading says that in many other countries, people die at home.

■ Indiantown, Part One   page 117

1. Answers will vary. It's all right if your question was not answered. Asking a question still helps you read more carefully.

2. b. The soldiers did not say they were innocent, so *a* is wrong. The soldiers did not say they were trying to leave Guatemala, so *c* is wrong.

3. walk to Mexico

4. The family worked long hours. They had no water. There was no school.

5. Answers will vary.

■ Indiantown, Part Two   page 121

1. c. They heard the army was still killing people in Guatemala.

2. The family was hungry and thirsty. The man gave them water, fruit, and candies.

3. a. 1; **b.** 4; **c.** 2; **d.** 3. Check the story if you do not have the right order.

4. Answers will vary.

■ Indiantown, Part Three   page 125

1. to pick fruit and vegetables

2. b. Isabela says, "Whatever we earn is usually spent on rent, food, and clothing."

3. Answers will vary. Store owners may charge more because they think migrant workers won't complain. Some workers may be afraid to complain because they are not here legally.

4. c. Since they have a washing machine, they don't have to wash clothes in the river.

5. They have found a peaceful place. They can go to church. They can work. No one is trying to kill them.

■ **End-of-Book Test: The Flying Africans   page 132**

1. b. The story says Africans lost their wings when they were "taken for slavery."

2. b. The Driver whipped her *after* she fell, so *a* is wrong. She did not fall when she tried to fly, so *c* is also wrong.

3. by saying magic words and holding out his arms

4. Answers will vary. He probably laughed because he knew he could fly away.

5. The Africans wanted to fly away because they were slaves. They were being worked to death. They wanted to be free.

6. Answers will vary. When the people flew away, it could also mean that they died.

To the Teacher

The *Foundations* Series

The *Foundations for Adult Reading* series was designed to do just what
the name states: lay a sound basis for reading comprehension in adult
new readers. It can be used on its own, as the core text in a reading
program that takes a whole-language approach. It can also be used as
part of a beginning reading program that includes decoding instruction.
The books assume students have an understanding of sound-symbol relationships, some decoding ability, and a basic sight-word reading vocabulary. This section provides information and suggests activities for teachers
working one-on-one with students as well as in a group situation.

High-Interest Readings on Adult Topics

The focus of the *Foundations* series is on building comprehension by
reading high-interest stories and using effective reading strategies. Each
book is organized around four themes: People, Coping, Messages, and
Cultures.

Unit 1, "People," depicts the life experiences of real people. The
variety of people represented reflects the multiethnic, multiracial nature
of our society. All of the people described have one quality in common:
they have made a significant contribution to society, sometimes in surprising ways.

Unit 2, "Coping," provides insights into how people cope with practical and emotional problems in their lives. Some of the articles, such as
"How to Save Money," discuss practical solutions to contemporary problems. Others, such as Robert Frost's poem "Stopping by Woods on a
Snowy Evening," are more contemplative and address the emotional side
of life.

The readings in Unit 3, "Messages," have to do with communication.
They tell about people who have a message to share with the rest of us.
Students are given opportunities to share their own messages through
speaking and writing.

The last unit, "Cultures," offers fictional and real-life stories that
express the richness of the multiple cultures of Americans. Folktales,

such as "The Flying Africans," speak in mythical terms of some of the deepest concerns of humans everywhere. The experiences of the most recent groups of immigrants to the United States, Asians and Hispanics, are told in "Rice and Rose Bowl Blues," "Ways of Dying," and "Indiantown." Students are also given the opportunity to reflect on traditions from their own cultural backgrounds.

Readability

Some people feel readability formulas are helpful in assessing materials; others do not. The Spache readability formula was one of many factors used to assess the lessons and reading passages in the *Foundations* books. Using the Spache formula, the approximate grade-equivalent reading level for *Foundations for Adult Reading 1* is mid first grade. The approximate grade-equivalent reading level for *Foundations for Adult Reading 2* is early second grade.

Readability formulas can be a useful tool for comparing reading material, as long as they are understood to be only a rough guideline. Assigning a grade level to reading material for adults can be misleading because adults are not at the same developmental level and do not have the same oral vocabulary as children. Whether a particular reading will be understood depends to a large part on the background knowledge the reader brings to the text. Grade levels, therefore, are one factor in evaluating the readability of a book, but certainly not the only factor.

Readability was also improved in the *Foundations* books by keeping lessons brief, breaking up text with illustrations, and designing the books with beginning adult readers in mind. The clarity of the writing style and the appeal of the subject matter also help determine the difficulty or ease with which a reader handles written material. The *Foundations* books offer a wide variety of subjects and themes. You may want to give students choices by letting them decide which reading passages or units to read.

Foundations and the *Adult Reading Comprehension* Series

Once students have completed the two *Foundations* books, you have the option of continuing their reading development with Scott, Foresman's *Adult Reading Comprehension* series. The themes in *Foundations*—People, Coping, Messages, and Cultures—are carried forward in *Adult Reading Comprehension,* as are the focus on building reading comprehension and the development of critical thinking.

Teaching Reading Strategies
with *Foundations*

Reading comprehension is a holistic process, not merely a composite of isolated skills. Comprehension improves as students develop *strategies* for approaching unfamiliar text. As these strategies become automatic, students become successful readers—regardless of whether they are reading on a second-grade level or a college level. A student who is a successful reader can read a story at his or her appropriate grade level, get meaning from it, respond to it, and add that meaning to a general framework of knowledge.

Foundations 2 encourages students to become "active readers"—readers who actively construct meaning from the text and respond to it in some way. The book teaches seven strategies and follows them up throughout the book.

The strategies taught in *Foundations 2* are described below, along with a listing of the pages on which they appear. Suggestions for teaching these strategies follow the descriptions.

Using What You Know

(pp. 4, 30, 38, 44, 47, 50, 58, 76, 106, 119, 130)

The beginning adult reader is far more likely to experience success with readings on familiar topics. By "using what they know," adult students can tap into the wealth of their personal experience.

However, some students are unable to make the connection between their personal knowledge and their reading. They may read a baseball story without ever applying what they already know about baseball to the story.

The strategy lesson "Using What You Know" on page 4 helps adult readers develop this ability by making the connection between prior knowledge and comprehension. Before reading a selection about the Mexican earthquake, students add what they already know about earthquakes to a word map. This strategy is followed up with mapping and listing activities in the "Before You Read" section of other selections as well.

Making Predictions Before
You Read

(pp. 9, 15, 55, 62, 92, 102, 110, 114, 117, 119)

Making predictions allows a reader to become actively engaged with the text. When readers begin to think about what an article could be about,

149

or what event could take place next in a story, they have a stronger purpose for reading and, thus, greater motivation to comprehend.

Emphasize to students that their predictions will not always be correct. Perhaps not enough information was given in the beginning for a good prediction. Or perhaps an author has deliberately misled the reader to create suspense. Remind students that the purpose of making predictions is to learn to look for clues about the topic of a reading and to think about the reading as it is being read.

The strategy lesson "Making Predictions Before You Read" on page 9 encourages students to make "good guesses" about the topic of a story or article. The "Before You Read" section for some selections also asks students to make predictions about the reading.

Finding the Main Idea

(pp. 42–43, 44–45, 46)

Approaching main idea as a strategy rather than as an isolated skill encourages greater independence in beginning adult readers. With a strategies approach, readers are taught that identifying the main idea of a reading is a tool for understanding and remembering what is read.

This strategy is a crucial one for beginning adult readers, who may not be able to distinguish between relevant and irrelevant information. To reinforce the concept that recognizing the main idea is a tool, rather than an end in itself, use "real" text instead of isolated paragraphs. For example, students could bring in news articles for discussions on how finding the main idea can help them better understand the articles.

The strategy lesson "Finding the Main Idea" on page 42 provides a visual explanation of the relationship between the main idea and supporting details. In the story that follows, students are asked to identify the main idea of each paragraph and of the entire selection.

Picturing What You Read

(pp. 54, 56–57, 66, 123)

Much has been written about the benefits of visualization techniques in areas ranging from finance to sports. For the beginning adult reader, creating a vivid picture while reading is a way to make text more meaningful and enjoyable. Readers are also more likely to notice their comprehension errors if those errors interfere with or contradict an image they have mentally constructed.

In the strategy lesson "Picturing What You Read" on page 54, students are encouraged to form a picture in their minds by noticing details about what is seen in a story. Sidenotes in the accompanying story ask students to describe to themselves what is happening in each scene.

Asking Yourself Questions

(pp. 79, 80, 83, 84, 86, 87, 89, 114, 118)

Asking questions is another way readers become actively involved with a text. Readers who formulate questions before, during, and after reading are more likely to comprehend and recall the details of the reading. This may include questions about what is happening in a story or article, why it happens, how it is related to what the reader already knows, and what it means personally to the reader.

The strategy lesson "Asking Yourself Questions" on page 79 highlights the importance of asking questions about a reading. In the three-part selection that follows, students are asked to formulate questions before reading each part of the story and to report on the answers afterwards. Later selections also ask students to write down questions before reading.

Reading in Phrases

(pp. 90–91, 92)

One obstacle for many beginning readers is their tendency to deal with only one word at a time, progressing so slowly that by the time they finish, they lose the overall sense of a passage. Learning to read in phrases is a very useful strategy for these students.

In the strategy lesson "Reading in Phrases" on page 90, students are asked to observe the way spoken language naturally breaks into phrases. Next, they put lines after phrases in sentences from a previous story. In the selection that follows, students practice breaking up the text into meaningful phrases. Tell your students that there is no one "right" way to divide sentences into phrases. The important thing is to learn to read in meaningful groups of words.

Checking Your Reading

(pp. 109, 111–112, 129)

Good readers expect a reading to make sense. When it doesn't, they go back to figure out why. Poor readers, on the other hand, have often experienced text that doesn't make sense. When they encounter an inconsistency, they are likely to ignore it and to proceed without a clear understanding. Self-checking is therefore an important strategy for these readers.

The strategy lesson "Checking Your Reading" on page 109 reminds students that reading should make sense and suggests questions students can ask themselves when they run into a problem. In the selection that follows, sidenotes pose questions enabling students to check their understanding as they read through the story.

Teaching Reading Strategies

As you guide students through *Foundations 2,* the following techniques will help you teach these strategies:

1. *Direct instruction.* The first time a strategy appears in *Foundations 2,* explain *what* it is, *how* it is helpful, and *when* it should be applied. Relate each strategy to examples from "real world" reading material—newspapers, magazines, job application forms, etc. When students read these materials, remind them of strategies that may help their comprehension.

2. *Teacher modeling.* As you move through the book, you can review strategies by *modeling* them for students.

Modeling is a four-step process. In the first step, you name the strategy and relate its usefulness to a concrete experience in the students' lives. In the second step, you define the strategy and model it by "thinking out loud" for the students. In step three, you assist students as they practice applying the strategy to another example. In step four, students practice the strategy independently.

Here is an example of a teacher modeling the "Asking Yourself Questions" strategy (p. 79) after reading "Mothers and Gangs, Part One" on pages 81–82.

Step 1   If you got a wedding invitation in the mail, you would probably ask yourself some questions about it. Can you think of some questions you'd ask? First, you'd probably want to know who was getting married! Then you might ask yourself, "What time is the service? Where is it? Am I invited to the reception?" You'd read the invitation to find the answers.

Step 2   When you ask yourself questions about what you read, you can understand and remember it better. I'll show you what I mean. Let's imagine I haven't read "Mothers and Gangs." What questions could I ask about the story before I read it? Let's see—the story is about gangs and there's a photograph of some boys near an abandoned building. I wonder what their lives are like? That can be one of my questions. As I read this story, I'm going to look for the answer.

After I read the story, I know more about those boys.

Step 3   Now, can you think of another question I could have asked about this story? (Possible answer: How do mothers feel when their sons join gangs? What can a mother do to help her sons stay out of gangs?)

Step 4   OK, now it's your turn. Look at "Chief Joseph's Surrender Speech" on pages 92–94. What are some questions you can ask yourself about the reading? (Possible question: What does the map show?) When you finish it, check and see if your questions are answered.

As students learn the different strategies, encourage them to make decisions about which strategies to use. Emphasize that expert readers are flexible in deciding which strategies will be most helpful in a given situation. You can also extend their understanding by modeling strategies with materials students bring in to read.

Using *Foundations 2* in Your Classroom

Foundations 2 was developed to involve your students in the whole of language—in reading, speaking, listening, and writing. You can use the book to have your students read and think about interesting topics, talk about the ideas they've read about, and write about those ideas.

Reading

The "Before You Read" sections guide students through prereading strategies. Stress the importance of these prereading strategies. You can use the analogy of swimming: A swimmer wouldn't just dive into a pool headfirst without first checking the depth of the water. In the same way, a good reader doesn't just "dive" into reading material without first "testing the water" by looking at the titles and pictures, determining the topic, thinking of what he or she already knows about the topic, and so on.

Use the prereading strategies discussed in each "Before You Read" section as a starting point; expand on these strategies whenever possible. Ask students what they know about the topic beforehand, and try to relate the topic to students' interests.

Some readings or parts of readings may be too difficult for certain students. Pay attention to how students react to these readings in particular: "Grandma Moses," "Ways of Dying," and "Indiantown." These readings contain special vocabulary that may make them more difficult to read. Students may also experience difficulty reading about topics of which they have little knowledge. In such cases, you can read to the students while they follow along.

Guided reading is another method you can use with certain selections. Have students read a section or even just a paragraph at a time. Then ask specific questions about what they have read. Ask whether they have any questions. Also ask students to predict what will happen next. Discuss previous predictions and whether they were correct. Then have students read the next section or paragraph. Continue this way through the entire selection.

Guided reading is also a good way to address the communicative nature of punctuation. Stress to students that the author of the selection is using punctuation marks to tell them when to pause (comma) or stop (period) and when to "hear" a question being asked (question mark) or a statement being said strongly (exclamation point). Marks of punctuation can even help students hear someone's exact words (quotation marks).

Avoid having students read aloud in front of others, unless they volunteer to do so. Adult readers are often extremely sensitive about their reading ability. It's best to limit such oral reading to private diagnostic sessions with yourself.

Writing

Writing abilities may be quite limited in students at this level. Some may not be able to do the writing activities suggested in the book. You are in the best position to decide on an individual basis whether to assign such activities and to whom.

If a student cannot respond in writing, you can have the student dictate his or her answers for you to write down. Then the student can read the answers back. This sort of language experience activity would be especially useful with the critical thinking questions under "Think About It."

When students do write their answers, try to emphasize the ideas they have communicated and not mechanics such as spelling or capitalization. Beginning writers are often reluctant writers because they fear making mistakes in grammar or spelling; you can help students overcome their hesitation by postponing instruction in the mechanics of English until they feel more at ease when they write.

Working in pairs is one way to overcome uneasiness about writing and help foster a cooperative learning atmosphere. Having students work in pairs to write their answers may remove the tension over making a mistake and create friendly, helpful peer relationships. However, be sensitive to individual personalities when trying this technique. Some adults prefer to work alone and may be uncomfortable writing in pairs.

Speaking and Listening

Questions in the book marked with the symbol of a speaking person are meant to be answered orally. These questions are best answered verbally either because the answer is too involved for students to write out or because there is more than one right answer (or no "right" answer).

When students are verbally answering involved questions, write their
answers on the board or an overhead transparency. Note words students
use in their speaking vocabularies that they do not have in their reading
vocabularies. You may want students to add these words to their word
banks.

When students are answering questions with no clear-cut answers,
you can use the questions as discussion topics. If you are working with a
group of students, group discussions can make the readings come alive.
Using small-group or class discussion in this way increases students'
interest and adds variety to classroom routine.

Make sure students understand the question. Set a time limit for discussion. If you are dividing the class into small groups, a group size
between three and six students is good. Assign or have each group select
a spokesperson to share the group's ideas with the class.

Not all students are able to keep up with a group discussion. Some
adults do not comprehend oral information that comes flooding in
quickly from several sources. They may also become lost or confused
when several people talk at once or in quick succession. You can help
such students by joining their group and keeping an ongoing list of the
main points of the discussion on a chalkboard or flip chart.

Building Vocabulary

Foundations 2 stresses vocabulary development through use of context
clues while reading and through building a word bank. Try to give suffi-
cient time to "Reading a New Word" in Unit 1 and the first lesson of
each unit after that ("Learning New Words," "Using Clues to Read New
Words," and "Figure It Out!"). Each should take a whole lesson in itself
to help ensure that students develop this difficult but valuable reading
strategy.

The "Words to Know" section before each selection and the word
banks students create with these words help increase their sight vocabulary. You can work with these tools.

Develop a speaking and reading familiarity with the words in "Words
to Know" in these ways.

- Say the words so that students know how to pronounce them.

- Ask students if they can use the words in sentences, and write their
  responses on the board or an overhead transparency.

- The definition given for each word in "Words to Know" is the meaning
  it has in the reading that follows. Talk with students about other
  meanings a word might have.

155

Encourage students to add words they read and hear to their word banks, in addition to the words in "Words to Know." You can use students' word banks as a resource for vocabulary activities such as these.

- Write meanings for the words on cards and have students match the words with their definitions.
- Create cloze exercises by writing a sentence for each word with a blank where the word belongs, and have students pick the card with the word that fits in the blank.
- Have students work in pairs and use their word bank cards as flash cards.
- Ask students to sort their words into different categories. For example, have them classify the words according to their initial letters, and teach the sounds of initial consonants. Next, have students sort the cards into spelling patterns (such as words with *ea* or words with long vowel sounds and final silent *e*'s), and teach these sound patterns. Then have students sort the words according to their referents (such as "things" and "people").

Testing Comprehension

The questions after each reading selection will help you measure students' comprehension—both literal and inferential—of the material they have just read. As noted before, you can have students write their answers or dictate the answers to you. You can also help students compose their answers or model answers for them. Some multiple-choice questions have been included because they are often easier for writing-reluctant students to answer. Questions to be answered orally can be handled individually, in small groups, or as a class.

Some questions—those requiring inference or application—depend on the ability to "read between the lines" or use one's background knowledge. Help students understand that the answer isn't always "right there" on the page; they must sometimes think about what they've read, put different parts of the material together to draw a conclusion, or use what they already know to answer a question. There are several methods for teaching strategies for answering questions—analyzing the relationship between question and answer and figuring out how to locate the answer. The QAR approach is one such method.

With QAR (Question Answer Relationships) you help students analyze whether the answer to a question is "in the book" or "in my head." If it is "in the book," students must find it "right there" (in one sentence on the page) or "put it together" (take different text parts to find it). If the answer is "in my head," students must determine whether the needed information is between the "author and me" (take information the author gives you and infer from it) or whether it can be found "on my own" (take information from your experience and knowledge and apply it). If you are interested in learning more about the QAR approach, see Taffy Raphael's article listed in the bibliography at the end of this section.

You can use the reading selections and questions to develop in your students such question-answering strategies as these and thereby further students' reading comprehension.

Whole-Language Activities with the *Foundations* Books

The *Foundations* books are excellent resources for use in whole-language teaching. The following activities may be used with the books to infuse whole-language learning into your tutorial or classroom instruction.

Fostering Interaction

To break the ice so that the talk and ideas flow during instruction, you may want to try the following activities.

- **The Warm-up** Before reading a selection, read and talk about short, digestible bits of print that are related to it. For example, the painting entitled *The Old Oaken Bucket* could serve as a warm-up for the story about Grandma Moses. Look at the painting. Read its title. Talk about it. Break the ice and encourage your students to start thinking about what they will read.

Jokes, cartoons, sayings, newspaper clippings, short poems, photos, commercials, or "tidbits" from the book may be used as warm-ups. You can read these to your students or take turns reading with them—whatever is most comfortable and natural.

- **Old Favorites** Just because you read something once doesn't mean you have to be done with it. Occasionally have your students select favorite stories, poems, or portions of articles to reread. You can use this as an opportunity to discuss the selection in greater detail, pointing out certain features of language. For example, if your students choose to reread their favorite poems from *Foundations 2,* discuss the words that helped them create mental pictures. Explore synonyms and antonyms for these high-image words. Add some to the word bank.

Or if your students choose to reread a selection about a famous person, ask them to describe the qualities and character traits that may have contributed to the person's success.

Have them relate the list to themselves or people they know. You can also use these new ideas to expand the word maps that were developed in earlier lessons.

157

Facilitating Involvement

You can show your adult learners what successful readers do while reading by involving them in these strategies.

▪ **Reciprocal Questioning** When you use this strategy, you and your students take turns asking each other questions about the first few paragraphs of a selection. Begin by explaining that everyone will read the first paragraph of a selection silently. When finished reading, each person is to think of a question to ask about the paragraph. You then take turns asking your questions. Of course, students and teacher can look back to answer a question if they need to. Continue reading and taking turns asking questions for two or three more paragraphs. Then finish reading the selection in the usual manner.

Your aim in this strategy is to model question-asking so that your students will do this on their own as they read. As they become familiar with the strategy, they can practice with each other as well as with you. Sometimes the questions you and your students create can be written down and used as a kind of quiz for each other. If you are interested in learning more about reciprocal questioning, see the A. V. Manzo article listed in the bibliography.

▪ **Free Response** Another way to get your students actively involved while reading is to have them jot down what they are thinking as they read. Before they read a selection, ask them to mark certain places in the text where they will stop reading. Then have them read the selection. At the preselected stops, they should pause and write down ideas or questions they have. You can write down your own responses as you read the selection along with the students. When finished, share your thoughts with one another.

You can use these free responses as springboards for discussion. For example, you may note how the selection related to what your students already know and to their own lives. Or you may have students talk about information that surprised them or was new for them. You may also discuss the language of the selection, e.g., words that vividly described events or sentences that seemed confusing to your students.

Integrating New Ideas

To help your students make connections between their reading, their experiences, and new ideas, you may want to try these two integration activities.

▪ **Theme Units** Since *Foundations* is already organized by units ("People," "Coping," "Messages," and "Cultures"), you can highlight these as themes by adding two simple activities.

Consider using *theme launchers,* such as books (fiction and nonfiction), poems, learner experiences, objects, or pictures to add information to the theme. These become an interesting way for learners to connect what they already know to new information they will encounter in the selections. For example, theme launchers for Unit 1, "People," might include newspaper clippings about current political figures, biographical sketches of famous people, or a family photo album. Those for the unit on "Coping" may involve informational brochures on health issues, recipes for special diets, or a calorie chart. Consider keeping theme launchers in a box or a scrapbook to add to or review occasionally.

Graphic organizers can also be used to show connections between different selections in a unit, making a theme more apparent. You can do this easily by expanding on the maps and charts that are included in many of the *Foundations* lessons.

For example, on page 113 of Unit 4, "Cultures," students map what they know about life in the United States. Expand the maps throughout the unit by having your students add new cultures and ideas after they read each selection. Draw on the backgrounds of your students to add other cultures to the map. As their maps enlarge, have them look for categories of information and create labels for them. For instance, students may develop categories such as food, clothing, language, and religion. Consider combining individual student maps into one large group map that illustrates further the ideas related to the theme of "cultures." Areas of special interest could become individual or small-group projects that you and your students explore beyond the book.

▪ **Learning Logs** Learning logs help your students monitor and direct their own learning. Explain to your students that they are to keep a log in which they record what they learn. Tell them not to worry about spelling or grammar. To guide their responses, they can ask themselves questions, such as these: ▪ What did I learn today?   ▪ What puzzled or confused me?   ▪ What new words do I know?   ▪ What did I enjoy, dislike, or accomplish in class today?

Provide ten minutes after each instructional session for students to write in their logs. Collect the logs regularly. You can use the logs to see what needs to be reviewed or clarified. Write comments directly to students in the log entries. This starts a conversation about learning between you and the student. Logs can also become the basis for instruction and a way to link what students know to new information they are learning.

Consider some of these whole-language activities in your instruction. They not only develop reading and writing, but they also invite adult learners to use reading and writing as tools for learning.

159

Key to Pronunciation

Pronunciations for a few words appear in the *Foundations* books. The following key has been used. The syllable that bears the greatest emphasis when the word is spoken appears in capital letters. If the word is long enough to have a syllable that receives secondary emphasis, that syllable appears in small capitals.

The key shows how common word sounds are indicated by diacritical marks in *The World Book Dictionary* and in the Scott, Foresman dictionaries. The pronunciation key also shows examples of the *schwa*, or unaccented vowel sound. The schwa is represented by ə.

Letter or Mark	As in	Respelling		Example
a	hat, map	a	ALPHABET	AL fuh beht
ā	age, fa	ay	ASIA	AY zhuh
ã	care, air	ai	BAREBACK	BAIR bak
ä	father, far	ah	ARMISTICE	AHR muh stihs
ch	child, much	ch	CHINA	CHY nuh
e	let, best	eh	ESSAY	EHS ay
ē	equal, see,	ee	LEAF	leef
	machine, city		MARINE	muh REEN
ėr	term, learn,			
	sir, work	ur	PEARL	purl
i	it, pin, hymn	ih	SYSTEM	SIHS tuhm
ī	ice, five	y	OHIO	oh HY oh
		eye	IRIS	EYE rihs
k	coat, look	k	CORN	kawrn
o	hot, rock	ah	OTTAWA	AHT uh wuh
ō	open, go, grow,	oh	RAINBOW	RAYN boh
	château		TABLEAU	TAB loh
ô	order, all	aw	ORCHID	AWR kihd
			ALLSPICE	AWL spys
oi	oil, voice	oy	COINAGE	KOY nihj
			POISON	POY zuhn
ou	house, out	ow	FOUNTAIN	FOWN tuhn
s	say, nice	s	SPICE	spys
sh	she, abolition	sh	MOTION	MOH shuhn
u	cup, butter,	uh	STUDY	STUHD ee
	flood		BLOOD	bluhd
ù	full, put, wood	u	FULBRIGHT	FUL bryt
			WOOL	wul
ü	rule, move, food	oo	ZULU	ZOO loo
zh	pleasure	zh	ASIA	AY zhuh
ə	about, ameba	uh	BURMA	BUR muh
	taken, purple	uh	FIDDLE	FIHD uhl
	pencil	uh	CITIZEN	SIHT uh zuhn
	lemon	uh	LION	LY uhn
	circus	uh	CYPRUS	SY pruhs
	labyrinth	uh	PHYSIQUE	fuh ZEEK
	curtain	uh	MOUNTAIN	MOWN tuhn
	Egyptian	uh	GEORGIA	JAWR juh
	section	uh	LEGION	LEE juhn
	fabulous	uh	ANONYMOUS	uh NAHN uh muhs

From *The World Book Encyclopedia*. © 1989 World Book, Inc. Used with permission.

Bibliography

Altwerger, Bess; Edelsky, Carole; and Flores, Barbara M. "Whole Language: What's New." *The Reading Teacher* 40 (November 1987):144–154.

Bacon, M. "What Adult Literacy Teachers Need to Know About Strategies for Focusing on Comprehension." *Lifelong Learning: The Adult Years,* vol. 6, no. 6 (1983):4–5.

Barasovska, Joan. *Getting Started with Experience Stories.* Syracuse, NY: New Readers Press, 1988.

Bowren, Faye R., and Zintz, Miles V. *Teaching Reading in Adult Basic Education.* Dubuque, IA: William C. Brown, 1977.

Carpenter, Tracy. *The Right to Read Tutor's Handbook for the SCIL (Student Centered Individualized Learning) Program.* Toronto: Frontier College, 1986.

Colvin, Ruth J., and Root, Jane H. *TUTOR: Techniques Used in the Teaching of Reading,* 6th ed. Syracuse, NY: Literacy Volunteers of America, 1987.

Cross, Kathryn Patricia. *Adults as Learners: Increasing Participation and Facilitating Learning.* San Francisco: Jossey-Bass, 1981.

Davidson, Jane L., and Wheat, Thomas E. "Successful Literacy Experiences for Adult Illiterates." *Journal of Reading* 32 (January 1989):342–346.

Duffy, Gerald G., et al. "Modeling Mental Processes Helps Poor Readers Become Strategic Readers." *The Reading Teacher* 41 (April 1988):762–767.

Fingeret, Arlene. *Adult Literacy: Current and Future Directions.* ERIC Clearinghouse on Adult, Career, and Vocational Education. The National Center on Research in Education, Ohio State University, 1984 (ERIC Document Reproduction Service No. ED 246 308).

Flood, James, ed. *Promoting Reading Comprehension.* Newark, DE: International Reading Association, 1984.

Forester, Anne D. "Learning to Read and Write at 26." *Journal of Reading* 31 (April 1988):604–613.

Fountas, Irene C., and Hannigan, Irene L. "Making Sense of Whole Language: The Pursuit of Informed Teaching." *Childhood Education,* Spring 1989, pp. 133–137.

Freire, Paulo. *Pedagogy of the Oppressed.* New York: Herder and Herder, 1970.

Goodman, Kenneth. *What's Whole in Whole Language?* Portsmouth, NH: Heinemann, 1986.

Hatch, Evelyn. "Reading a Second Language." In *Teaching English as a Second or Foreign Language.* New York: Newbury House Publishers, 1979.

Heathington, B. S. "Expanding the Definition of Literacy for Adult Remedial Readers." *Journal of Reading* 31 (December 1987):213–217.

Heilman, Arthur. *Phonics in Proper Perspective.* Columbus, OH: Charles E. Merrill, 1985.

Hermann, Beth Ann. "Two Approaches for Helping Poor Readers Become More Strategic." *The Reading Teacher* 42 (October 1988):24–28.

Johnson, Dale D., and Pearson, P. David. *Teaching Reading Vocabulary.* New York: Holt, Rinehart and Winston, 1984.

Jones, Edward V. *Reading Instruction for the Adult Illiterate.* Chicago: American Library Association, 1981.

Kazemek, Francis E., and Rigg, Pat. "Four Poets: Modern Poetry in the Adult Literacy Classroom." *Journal of Reading* 30 (December 1986):218–225.

Knowles, Malcolm. *The Modern Practice of Adult Education: From Pedagogy to Androgogy,* 2nd ed. New York: Cambridge Book Co., 1980.

Knox, Alan B. *Adult Development and Learning.* San Francisco: Jossey-Bass, 1977.

Lane, Martha A., ed. *Handbook for Volunteer Reading Aides.* Philadelphia: Lutheran Church Women, 1984.

Manzo, A. V. "The Request Procedure." *Journal of Reading* 11 (1969):123–126.

Mayes, Cheryl. "Five Critical Thinking Strategies for Adult Basic Education Learners." *Lifelong Learning* 10 (May 1987):11–13, 25.

McNeil, John D. *Reading Comprehension: New Directions for Classroom Practice.* 2nd ed. Glenview, IL: Scott, Foresman and Company, 1987.

Meyer, Valerie, and Keefe, Donald. *Reading for Meaning: Selected Teaching Strategies.* Lifelong Learning Books Teacher Resource Series. Glenview, IL: Scott, Foresman and Company, 1990.

Mocker, Donald W., ed. *Teaching Reading to Adults.* Scott, Foresman/AAACE Adult Educator Series. Glenview, IL: Scott, Foresman and Company, 1986.

Norman, C., and Malicky, G. "Stages in the Reading Development of Adults." *Journal of Reading* 30 (January 1987):302–307.

Ottoson, Gerald, et al. *Tutoring Small Groups: Basic Reading.* Syracuse, NY: Literacy Volunteers of America, 1985.

Padak, Gary M., and Padak, Nancy D. "Guidelines and a Holistic Method for Adult Basic Reading Programs." *Journal of Reading* 30 (March 1987): 490–496.

Palmieri, Mary Ann De Vita. "Julie: A Special Kind of Illiteracy." *Lifelong Learning* 12 (October 1988):7–9.

Pearson, P. David. "Changing the Face of Reading Comprehension." *The Reading Teacher* 38 (April 1985):724–738.

Perin, Dolores. "Schema Activation, Cooperation and Adult Literacy Instruction." *Journal of Reading* 32 (October 1988):54–62.

Pinell, Gay Su, and Matlin, Myrna. *Teachers and Research: Language Learning in the Classroom.* Newark, DE: International Reading Association, 1989.

Raphael, Taffy E. "Teaching Question Answer Relationships, Revisited." *The Reading Teacher* 39 (February 1986):516–522.

Rauch, Sidney J., and Sanacore, J., eds. *Handbook for the Volunteer Tutor.* 2nd ed. Newark, DE: International Reading Association, 1985.

Rice, Gail. *Preparing Your Own ABE Adult Basic Education Reading Materials.* Lifelong Learning Books Teacher Resource Series. Glenview, IL: Scott, Foresman and Company, 1990.

Rigg, Pat, and Kazemek, Francis. "For Adults Only: Reading Materials for Adult Literacy Students." *Journal of Reading* 28 (May 1985):728–731.

Rosenthal, Nadine. *Teach Someone to READ: A Step-by-Step Guide for Literacy Tutors.* Belmont, CA: Fearon/David S. Lake Publishers, 1987.

Scales, Alice, and Burley, Jo Anne. "A Holistic Approach to Teaching Adult Literacy Techniques." *Lifelong Learning* 12 (November 1988):26–28.

Shuman, R. Baird. "Some Assumptions About Adult Reading Instruction." *Journal of Reading* 32 (January 1989):348–354.

Smith, Frank. *Reading Without Nonsense.* 2nd ed. New York: Teacher's College Press, 1985.

Tierney, Robert J.; Readence, John E.; and Dishner, Ernest K. *Reading Strategies and Practices, A Compendium,* 2nd ed. Newton, MA: Allyn and Bacon, 1985.

Weaver, Constance. *Reading Process and Practice: From Socio-Psycholinguistics to Whole Language.* Portsmouth, NH: Heinemann, 1988.